Transnational Migration

Immigration and Society series

Thomas Faist, Margit Fauser and Eveline Reisenauer,
Transnational Migration

Grace Kao, Elizabeth Vaquera and Kimberly Goyette,
Education and Immigration

Christian Joppke, *Citizenship and Immigration*

Ronald L. Mize and Grace Peña Delgado, *Latino Immigrants in
the United States*

Philip Q. Yang, *Asian Immigration to the United States*

Transnational Migration

*Thomas Faist, Margit Fauser and
Eveline Reisenauer*

polity

First published in 2013 by Polity Press

Polity Press
65 Bridge Street
Cambridge CB2 1UR, UK

Polity Press
350 Main Street
Malden, MA 02148, USA

ISBN-13: 978-0-7456-4977-1
ISBN-13: 978-0-7456-4978-8(pb)

A catalogue record for this book is available from the British Library.

Typeset in 11 on 13 pt Sabon
by Servis Filmsetting Ltd, Stockport, Cheshire

The publisher has used its best endeavours to ensure that the URLs for external websites referred to in this book are correct and active at the time of going to press. However, the publisher has no responsibility for the websites and can make no guarantee that a site will remain live or that the content is or will remain appropriate.

Every effort has been made to trace all copyright holders, but if any have been inadvertently overlooked the publisher will be pleased to include any necessary credits in any subsequent reprint or edition.

For further information on Polity, visit our website: www.politybooks.com

Contents

v

Contents

Contents

Preface and Acknowledgements

Increasing interconnections between nation-states across borders have made the transnational perspective a key tool for understanding our world. It has made particularly strong contributions to immigration studies and holds great promise for deepening insights into international migration. This book provides an accessible yet rigorous overview of cross-border migration from a transnational perspective – as experienced by family and kinship groups, networks of entrepreneurs, diasporas and immigrant associations, and as regulated by states. As well as defining the core concepts of transnationalization, transnational social spaces and transnationality, we describe everyday transnational life, explore the implications for immigrant integration, and take a fresh look at issues of membership and citizenship. By examining the political, economic, social and cultural dimensions of transnational migration, we seek to capture the distinctive features of the new immigrant communities that have reshaped the ethno-cultural mix of receiving nations, including the US and Western Europe. Importantly, we also examine the effects of transnationality on regions of migrants' origin, viewing migrants as agents of political and economic development. In doing so, we aim to balance theoretical discussion with relevant examples and cases, making this an ideal book for upper-level students covering immigration and transnational relations, in sociology, political science and globalization courses.

Various persons have contributed to the successful completion of this project. We are especially grateful for the helpful comments of anonymous reviewers. We also wish to thank those whose efforts have helped to finish the book and whose work usually does not get to be seen. We wish to thank the students from a graduate-level course at the Department of Sociology at Bielefeld University for reading and critically discussing draft chapters. Their suggestions and questions greatly improved the readability. Edith Klein and Caroline Richmond have carefully edited the manuscript for publication. Eva Drebenstedt helped us in preparing the manuscript. The Polity Press team – Jonathan Skerrett, India Darsley and Sarah Dobson – has also been very supportive. We are grateful to all of them.

We are especially grateful to the Collaborative Research Centre 882 'From Heterogeneities to Social Inequalities' at Bielefeld University for supporting the preparation of this book.

Thomas Faist, Margit Fauser and Eveline Reisenauer

1

Three Transnationals: Transnationalization, Transnational Social Spaces and Transnationality

To say 'international migration' is to say 'cross-border connections' or the ties and practices of migrants and non-migrants linking countries of emigration and immigration – that is, the connections between those who leave, those who stay behind and those who do not move are a salient aspect of the migration experience. The connections between the places of origin and destination, and of onward and return movements, are an integral component of migration. A transnational perspective means that migration is not an irrevocable process but may entail repeated movements and, above all, continued transactions – bounded communication between actors – between migrants and non-migrants across the borders of states. Cross-border migration inherently generates cross-border ties and practices: letters, phone calls, visits, family remittances and economic investments in migrants' communities of origin yield feedback spurring additional departures and manifold changes in the regions where they and their significant others live.

This book takes a decidedly cross-border perspective on international migration. A transnational perspective goes beyond the usual preoccupation of immigration researchers, who, in focusing mainly on countries of immigration, assume that state and (civil) society normally converge. But simply adding on the emigration country experience, or connections of immigrants to their places of origin, is not enough. Instead, our perspective suggests adopting a third way, one that takes the multi-sitedness of migrants seriously. The

1

transnational perspective shows that people, social groups, net-works, communities and organizations frequently operate beyond the borders of nominally sovereign states. A transnational perspective on migration – and this is what we mean by transnational migration – focuses on how the cross-border practices of migrants and non-migrants, individuals as well as groups and organizations, link up in social spaces criss-crossing national states, mould economic, political and cultural conditions, and are in turn shaped by already existing structures. The 'transnational' has three components. First, migrants' ties are embedded in broader processes of *transnationalization* – that is, the processes involving transnational ties and practices in various fields, including the cross-border transactions of goods, services, capital and ideas and the movement of people. Second, the transactions of migrants and other agents across borders result in social formations we call *transnational social spaces*. These social spaces take various forms, including kinship groups, circuits and communities. Third, individuals and groups engage in a continuum of cross-border transactions ranging from activities such as travelling, exchanging goods and services, and sending and receiving remittances to communicating ideas back and forth. It is thus *transnationality*, the degree of connectivity between migrants and non-migrants across national borders, which becomes important. While nation-states shape both the movements of people across borders and their transnationality, they determine neither all movement back and forth nor the form taken by the life worlds of migrants.

The film by the German-Turkish director Fatih Akın entitled *The Edge of Heaven* (*Auf der anderen Seite*) offers an instructive entry into transnational life worlds (Ezli 2010). It tells of people who cross the national borders of Germany and Turkey but also cross boundaries between families, ethnically self- and other-defined majority and minority groups and generations. It is not a matter simply of one-way movement from one country to another but of various movements intersecting borders in both directions. Aytin, who lives in Turkey, and whose mother, Yeter, is based in the city of Bremen in Germany, gets into trouble because of her engagement with Kurdish nationalism. She travels to Germany in search of her mother. In the port city of Hamburg, she befriends Lotte, a university student. When Aytin is denied asylum by the German authorities and is sent back to Turkey, Lotte sets out to Istanbul to support her friend. Nejat, the son of a former 'guest worker', Ali Aksu from Bremen, is a successful 'second-generation' child who succeeded in becoming a university professor of German literature. Nonetheless, he leaves his position in Hamburg and takes over a bookshop in Istanbul. This shop, interestingly enough, is not a Turkish one, but one offering German-language books. He moves the geographical locus of his life from Germany to Turkey: in his case it is not simply a return to the country of origin, as would be denoted by the term 'second-generation return'. The movements of these and other protagonists in the film are not tales of return in the classical sense. Even coffins cross borders in transit in both directions. Yeter, who dies in Bremen, is returned by Turkish Airlines to Istanbul, and Lotte, who is accidentally shot by street children, is returned by Lufthansa from Istanbul to Hamburg. They inhabit what might be called transnational social spaces. They live and die transnationally.

The film depicts not only ties across the borders of countries or nations but also mobility across generations. Nejat, representing the second generation of Turkish immigrants in Germany, is a successful university professor who does not follow a standard integration path predicted by sociological integration theories. Common wisdom has it that, with rising educational credentials and success, an individual's orientation to their parents' country of origin declines. Yet Nejat's story defies this prediction. Also, Lotte, the daughter of Susanne, is engaged in helping her friend Aytin, a political refugee. In order to do so she has to break with her mother, who clearly belongs to the 'generation of 1968'. Lotte ventures to Istanbul against the wishes of her mother. Yet, with her political engagement, Lotte continues in her mother's political path. In short, there is no linear logic connecting the first generation to the second or the country of emigration to that of immigration.

The crossing of borders and boundaries is also not coterminous with intercultural communication or dialogue, or with a celebration of cultural diversity as enrichment. When Susanne searches for her daughter, she eventually meets up with Nejat in his Istanbul apartment. Looking out of the window, the two of them watch people going to the mosque to observe Kurban Bayramı (the festival of sacrifice). Susanne asks Nejat why this holiday is observed. Nejat then tells her the story of Abraham's sacrifice according to the Qur'an. Susanne responds that the same story could be found in the Bible. One might now expect that an intercultural dialogue would ensue on the different interpretations of this episode in the Muslim and Christian traditions. Yet this is not the case. The two figures stand not for different cultures but for persons with similar life stories who happen to meet, suggesting that it is not a fixed or even a hyphenated identity which occupies the foreground. Rather, what is at stake are the connectivities and ties between people and across generations, families, religions and states.

Throughout, the film traces the trajectories of the characters and their ties – which cross national borders and generational boundaries – without losing sight of the importance of national states to their lives. The film's approach does not correspond to known metaphors describing the migration experience as the uprooting and transplanting of people into a new environment. It is no classical tale of loss of home, estrangement, foreignness, rootlessness and marginalization, or a film in which migrants celebrate the culture(s) they brought with them to their new homeland. Instead, it deals with continuous delocalization and relocalization in a transnational world which cannot be reduced to contexts of emigration and immigration. *The Edge of Heaven* depicts cross-border connections, as well as biographical and family connections, which reach across generations. The life world of the protagonists is neither German nor Turkish, nor even simply an overlap between the two – it is a third social world. This is the perspective we as researchers take in this book.

We offer a comprehensive analytical framework for understanding cross-border migration and its consequences from a transnational point of view. It is a building block towards a coherent theory of transnationalization, here focusing on migration. This introductory chapter contains three parts. First, we sketch the phenomenon with which transnational ties and structures are connected and discussed in this book – that is, cross-border migration – and explain why a transnational perspective helps to account for processes so far poorly understood. Second, we define the key terms used, disaggregating the broad and sweeping term 'transnational' into three analytically useful concepts – namely, transnationalization, transnational social spaces and transnationality. And, third, we discuss the rationale and aims of the book and introduce the questions discussed in the individual chapters.

Cross-border migration and the need for a transnational perspective

International or, more precisely, cross-border migration is here understood to mean a change of residence from one country to another over a meaningful period of time. And we hasten to add, from a transnational perspective, that even a change of residence may not be simply unidirectional but may involve movement back and forth, and that settlement does not necessarily imply a severing of ties to the place of origin. This book concerns international rather than domestic or internal migrants, although the latter are much more numerous, and the focus is on South–North migration and not South–South migration, which probably involves even more people. Thus the book deals explicitly with a particular aspect of the migration experience. The overwhelming majority of people who move do so within the borders of their own country (UNDP 2009: 21). According to the International Organization for Migration, there were about 214 million international migrants in the early twenty-first century – a number that marks a rapid increase over the last few decades (IOM 2009: 1). By contrast, the 2001 census in India showed that there were 309 million internal migrants in the country (Bhagat 2009: 4), while the 2000 Chinese census counted 144 million domestic migrants in China (Ha et al. 2009: 7). Among the poorest populations, migration takes place primarily within and between developing countries. For example, many countries in South-East Asia rely heavily on cheap migrant labour from neighbouring countries – for example, Malaysia has a large number of Indonesian workers. As for refugees, four-fifths live in developing countries and more than a third dwell in the least developed countries.[1] Nonetheless, over the past decades, the proportion of international migrants relative to domestic migrants has increased. Of the former, about half – circa 74 million – of all international migrants move between so-called developing countries. This estimate is likely to be too low, as the official data tend to undercount irregular migrants. Irregular migration is probably even more common in between countries in the South than from South to North (World Bank 2008: 3; Bakewell 2009: 17).[2] If we disaggregate these figures among world regions and look at them from a chronological perspective, we realize that cross-border migration is unevenly distributed across the globe. We can also see that there has been a slow but steady rise in the proportion of the world's population who are migrants – from about 2 per cent in 1960 to between 3 and 4 per cent in 2010.

A transnational approach is needed to make sense of tendencies in international migration which have not hitherto been at the centre of analysis. It takes seriously the observation that migrants do not usually break off their contacts with their countries and communities of origin upon settlement in new countries; rather, we see that they often maintain ties to significant others and even forge new ones. For example, a survey of selected migrant groups from Latin America in three cities in the US carried out in the 1990s found that a significant minority maintain strong transnational political, cultural and economic ties (Portes 2003). They are engaged in such cross-border practices as following political affairs in their country of origin and sending remittances on a regular basis. Similar conclusions can be drawn from data from the German Socio-Economic Panel on cross-border (financial) transactions among migrants in Germany, which suggest that a tenth to a third of all migrants can be defined as transnational, depending on the benchmarks set for the regularity and intensity of such transactions (Holst et al. 2012). Such ties may extend back to the regions of origin but also to other countries in which significant others have settled. A particularly good example is migrants from Turkey who have settled in substantial numbers in such European countries as Germany, France and the Netherlands while retaining significant ties across the regions of immigration (Abadan-Unat 2011). A transnational perspective also takes heed of the fact that people are spatially mobile and may not settle in the countries in which they work – for example, those engaged in seasonal work or in posted workers' arrangements (Faist 1997). In a nutshell, a transnational approach recognizes the multi-stranded and cross-border ties of individuals, groups and organizations and their sometimes simultaneous engagement across the borders of national states. Such transactions may refer to intra-family financial support, on one side of the spectrum, and the activities of nationalist diasporas, on the other. What makes cross-border migration such a suitable site for exploring transnational processes is the fact that we can observe how individuals, groups and organizations actually engage in transactions across borders of national states not only with respect to their life worlds but also in fields such as education, the labour market and politics.

Unpacking the transnational

The transnational approach was born out of the observation that migrants do not simply cross borders to live elsewhere but may turn this into a strategy of survival and betterment – indeed, into a lifestyle of its own. That we observe such developments more intensively today – although it is not a totally new phenomenon (chapter 3) – is perhaps not all that surprising considering that present-day migration takes place in a world characterized by the compression of time and space (Harvey 1990). Air travel has become cheaper than ever before and staying in touch, because of technological developments such as the Internet, has never been so easy. Notwithstanding the presence of international borders and all the laws and regulations imposed by national states on those wishing to cross them, transnational relationships have intensified.

Two uses of the term 'transnational' need to be distinguished. The first is very loose, denoting any kind of cross-border transaction, even fleeting ones such as a tourist trip abroad. When we use the term in a narrower and more specific sense – which is the one used in this book – we refer to a process by which migrants forge and sustain multi-stranded social relations that link together their societies of origin and settlement. Many migrants today build social spaces which span political, geographical, and cultural borders (Basch et al. 1994).

Note that cross-border migration is not the only context in which sustained transnational ties may emerge. Such ties may be found among national minorities and those in their original kin state – for example, the large numbers of 'ethnic' Hungarians who have been living outside Hungary for centuries in what today are Slovakia and Romania. It makes a difference whether the relationship with an external homeland has come about through the movement of people across borders, as in migration, or of changes in borders as a result of war settlements, as is the case with the Hungarians. And it also makes a difference whether the situation in the host country is that immigrants have arrived recently and become territorially dispersed or that a settled minority has lived continuously in a particular territory over many generations and may even enjoy cultural minority rights. Additional sites of research are cross-border social movements (della Porta and Tarrow 2005), advocacy networks in the fields of human rights or the environment (Keck and Sikkink 1998), networks of criminal gangs and organizations (Shelley 1995), civil society organizations in the area of social and labour standards (Faist 2009) and religious communities (Levitt 2007). In all of these cases it is not primarily migrants who forge and entertain transnational ties and practices but relatively immobile persons and organizations who communicate and exchange ideas and goods across borders.

Another remark on terminology is in order. When the word 'transnational' was first used specifically in migration studies, in the early 1990s, the term 'transnationalism' was very prominent (Basch et al. 1994). Yet this latter term conflates the ideas of 'state' and 'nation', the first referring to territorial units, the second to social collectives. By definition, cross-border migration connects the territorial units of the global. However, 'state' and 'nation' may not necessarily be coterminous. There are quite a few state-less nations around the globe. Therefore, in earlier work, Thomas Faist used the term 'trans-state' to refer to the territorial fact of cross-border migration, and 'trans-national' to refer to collectives (Faist 2000b). Few scholars have attended to the matter (see, however, Fox 2005: 172). In this book, we will not differentiate semantically between these two terms and will continue to use, as do virtually all authors, 'transnational' for cross-border – that is, 'trans-state'. Yet we will indicate at which level of aggregation the ties and practices refer to collectives, such as family or house-hold, network, organization, local community (hence the term trans-local) or state. Therefore 'transnational' is a catch-all term which must be disaggregated in various ways to be of use. The subsequent analysis will refer to these terms and not 'transnation-alism', which suggests an ideology. However, it is not clear whose ideology it would connote: that of researchers, migrants, other observers – or all of these?

Transnational approaches certainly do not (yet) form a coher-ent theory or set of theories. They can more adequately be described as a perspective which has found entry into the study of manifold cross-border phenomena. We can delineate three key concepts of transnational scholarship relevant for migration research: transnationalization, transnational social spaces and transnationality. Interestingly, they correspond to three succeed-ing generations of research: transnationalization for theories of 'transnational relations' in the political science field of inter-national relations in the 1960s and 1970s, transnational social spaces in sociology and anthropology from the latter part of the 1990s onwards and, finally, transnationality as a new concept which we seek to put forward. Nonetheless, these concepts have not replaced each other. All three are vital for a transnational research programme.

Three Transnationals

Transnationalization as cross-border processes

A transnational approach is not a coherent theory but a lens. It looks at cross-border transactions as a process, namely transnationalization, which refers to sustained ties, events and activities across the borders of several nation-states. It focuses above all on non-state agents. Nonetheless, states also participate in seeking to regulate borders, places of residence, economic activity and access to rights. The Oxford Dictionary of English dates the emergence of the term 'transnational' to around 1920, documented with a quotation from an economic text that characterized Europe after the First World War by its 'international or more correctly transnational economy'. The term re-emerged only in the late 1960s in what was called transnational relations in the field of international relations to denote increasing economic and political interdependence between industrialized countries, referring to processes which involve powerful non-state actors such as multinational companies and, to a lesser extent, political parties such as the Socialist International. Transnational relations in political science pointed beyond state-centrism and the billiard-ball models of international relations and asked about the emergence, role and impact on states and international organizations of large-scale, cross-border, non-state organizations (Keohane and Nye 1977). Curiously, the interest in this approach disappeared with the onset of debates on globalization from the late 1970s onwards. Perhaps its demise was related to the fact that globalization studies, taking a 'top-down' view, recentred interest on how national state political economies were reshaped by ever growing capital flows across borders. Nonetheless, there have continually been scholars who are interested in how transnational practices, such as networks of capitalists, shape the current world (Sklair 2001).

Clearly, transnationalization is different from internationalization, the latter dealing with ties, events and processes involving exclusively states and their agents. An example of internationalization would be international regimes – for example, the order protecting refugees, based on the 1951 Geneva Convention and its subsequent protocols. Also, globalization differs from both transnationalization and internationalization in that it takes a bird's-eye view. This involves at least two aspects: first, the intensification of interdependence and interconnectedness around the globe (Giddens 1990) and, second, the emergence of a single global system, such as a new global state (Albrow 1996: 178). While the first aspect overlaps with transnationalization, the second is specific to globalization and world theories. These theories take world-spanning structures as a point of departure and ask how such structures and associated processes impact and shape lower-level structures and processes – for example, at the level of the nation-state and below. In a way, they move from the 'outside' towards the 'inside' and from the 'top' to the 'bottom'. In certain regional contexts globalization is reflected in more delimited developments, such as the rise of the European Union (EU). Often, the term is used to denote rapid and deregulated flows of capital that are restructuring patterns of investment, production, labour deployment and consumption. Ideas, technology and goods and services of all sorts are moving rapidly across the globe. Theorists of globalization, such as Ulrich Beck (1999), conceptualize the contemporary world by seeing the modernity of European societies upscaled to the world level. It is a perspective which assumes that European and North American modernity is globalized or generalized from a national state to a global level, as if these models of modernity – of political, cultural and economic development – could be generalized across the world. In short, they basically upscale nation-state theories.

A transnational approach, by contrast, suggests another take. Cross-border agency and structures can be understood only by examining the actual links between the parts of the world. This view holds that cross-border formations – or, indeed, even a world society – are constructed by cross-border practices, and that this implies a research agenda tracing such practices. A transnational approach starts with the very processes which constitute cross-border agency and structures, which are exemplified by the practices of migrants and non-migrants who forge ties across borders (Faist 2000a: 211). The focus on cross-border processes helps to open up a conceptual space which can be filled by the terms 'transnational social spaces' and 'transnationality', with concern about migrant networks, traders and ethnic business constellations, politics of place among migrants and returnees, diasporas and development, and migrant integration – but also social movements and advocacy networks.

Transnational social spaces as cross-border social structures

The pioneers of the transnational approach in migration research, Nina Glick Schiller and her associates, contended that there is something qualitatively different about immigrants today compared with their late nineteenth- and early twentieth-century counterparts. They viewed this earlier era's immigrants as having broken off all homeland social relations and cultural ties, thereby locating themselves solely within the socio-cultural, economic and political orbit of the receiving society. By contrast, according to Glick Schiller and her colleagues, today's immigrants are composed of those whose networks, activities and patterns of life encompass both societies, and they coined two new terms to capture this novelty: 'transnationalism' and 'transmigrants'. While the former refers to the process by which immigrants build social fields that link their country of origin and their country of settlement, the latter refers to the immigrants who build such social fields by maintaining a wide range of affective and instrumental social practices spanning borders. Instead of focusing on 'transnationalism from above' by looking at powerful agents such as multinational companies, as the transnational relations approach in international relations had done, their emphasis on 'transnationalism from below' tried to restore agency to what would appear from a macro-political view to be minor players – in this case, migrants: 'Transnational political, economic, social, and cultural processes (1) extend beyond borders of a particular state but are shaped by the policies and institutional practices of a particular and limited set of states; and (2) include actors that are not states' (Glick Schiller and Fouron 1999: 343–4). The transactions involved take the form of material one- or two-way transfers such as financial remittances or ideas but also concern the exchange of information.

In this perspective, the multiple identities of contemporary migrants are fluid; these identities reveal a resistance on the part of migrants to the global political and economic situations that engulf them. This insight necessitates rethinking received ideas regarding class, nationalism, ethnicity and race. An important implication of the discussion is that assimilation and cultural pluralism are inadequate to account for the distinctive character of contemporary migration. Whereas assimilation implies the loss of past identity, cultural pluralism advances an essentialist perspective that treats ethnic identities as immutable.

The pioneers of transnational research in the field of migration also contended that social science must become 'unbound'. The argument is that the problem with theories operating with closed systems in which the unit of analysis is ultimately the nation-state is that they fail to provide room for the wider field of action occupied by contemporary migrants. Glick Schiller and others stressed that transnationalization is the product of world capitalism, which has produced economic dislocations that make immigrants economically vulnerable. At the same time, migrants are not just passive objects but active shapers of their social world. Research then identified cross-border practices as sustained ties of individuals, networks and organizations, ranging from weak to strongly institutionalized forms. Transnational ties are not about fleeting contacts between migrants and relatively immobile people in the countries of origin and destination. On the contrary, this gaze at the 'global' in the 'local' dealt with dense and continuous ties across the borders of nation-states, which cluster into social formations called transnational social spaces. These spaces consist of combinations of ties and their contents, positions in networks and organizations, and networks of organizations that can be found in at least two nation-states. Most of these formations are located in between familial and personal practices, on the one hand, and the functional systems of differentiated spheres, such as the socio-cultural, economic and political, on the other. Transnational social spaces are dynamic social processes, definitely not static notions of ties and positions: 'By transnational spaces we mean relatively stable, lasting and dense sets of ties reaching beyond and across the borders of sovereign states. They consist of combinations of ties and their contents, positions in networks and organizations, and networks or organizations that cut across the borders of at least two nation-states. Transnational spaces differ from clearly demarcated state territories' (Faist 2000a: 197; see also Kivisto 2001). In other words, the term refers to sustained and continuous pluri-local transactions crossing state borders. The most basic element of transnational social formations is the transaction or tie – that is, a bounded communication between social agents such as individual persons. Regular practices concatenate into social structures. Agents in transnational social spaces may be individuals, groups or organizations and even states. It is an empirical question whether such cross-border transactions are global or only regional in scope.

There are three expressions of transnational spaces, which will be discussed in detail later in this book (chapter 3):

1 *Transnational kinship groups*, such as transnational families who conceive of themselves as both an economic unit and a unit of reciprocity and who keep, in addition to the primary home, a kind of shadow household in another country. Economic assets are mostly transferred from abroad to those who continue to run the household 'back home'.

2 *Transnational circuits* are sets of ties between people and organizations in which information and services are exchanged for the purpose of achieving a common goal. Linkage patterns may concatenate in advocacy networks, business networks or scientists' networks. These issue-specific circuits or networks engage in areas such as human rights and environmental protection.

3 *Transnational communities* comprise dense and continuous sets of social and symbolic ties, characterized by a high degree of intimacy, emotional depth, moral obligation and social cohesion. Geographical proximity is no longer a necessary criterion for the existence of a community – there are 'communities without propinquity'. Transnational communities can evolve at different levels of aggregation. The simplest type consists of village communities in transnational social spaces, whose

relations are marked by solidarity extended over long periods of time. The quintessential form of transnational communities consists of larger cross-border religious groups and churches. World religions – Judaism, Christianity, Islam, Hinduism and Buddhism – existed long before modern states came into existence. Diasporas also belong to the category of transnational communities. Diasporas are groups that experienced the territorial dispersion of their members at some time in the past, as a result either of a traumatic experience or specialization in long-distance trade (Cohen 1997). Transnational communities do not necessarily involve individual persons living in two worlds simultaneously or between cultures in a 'global village' of de-territorialized space. What is required, however, is that communities without propinquity link through solidarity to achieve a high degree of social cohesion through a common repertoire of symbolic and collective representations.

Transnationality as a marker of heterogeneity

Going a step further, we introduce a third key concept for transnational scholarship which is concerned above all with methodological questions: transnationality. With this addition we aim to contribute to the further development of a transnational theoretical framework. Transnationalization, as we have seen, sets the frame for sustained cross-border transactions of agents. Transnational social spaces, as defined above, refer to sustained concatenation of such cross-border ties and practices. So far, we have discussed studies which juxtaposed what were called transmigrants with classical international migrants – that is, emigrants, immigrants and return migrants. Depending on how migrants are defined, about a quarter of all Mexican migrants to the US may be classified as transnational – that is, having some sort of cross-border ties, such as sending remittances, travelling to the country of origin or keeping an interest in political affairs (Donato et al. 2010). But research in this vein has two problems. First, cross-border transactions are not either–or practices but often vary along a continuum from low to high (Faist et al. 2011). Second, such research has overemphasized the aspect of geographical mobility. The role of relatively immobile household or kinship members who enable cross-border migration in the first place, as well as the cross-border exchange of ideas and underlying symbolic ties, is not sufficiently considered. Not all individuals and groups who contribute to the formation of transnational ties in what we have called transnational social spaces regularly cross borders between two or more nation-states. It is not only recent migrants but also their sometimes immobile family members and also settled migrants who engage in transnational practices. Moreover, those who have not migrated and are not associated with migrants but are well connected to colleagues abroad through work-based conduits entertain cross-border transactions as well (Mau 2010).

This is why the concept 'transnationality' is helpful. Transnationality connotes the social practices of agents – individuals, groups, communities and organizations – across the borders of nation-states. The term denotes a spectrum of cross-border ties in various spheres of social life – familial, socio-cultural, economic and political – ranging from travel, through sending financial remittances, to exchanging ideas. Seen in this way, agents' transnational ties constitute a marker of heterogeneity, akin to other heterogeneities, such as age, gender, citizenship, sexual orientation, cultural preferences or language use. In short, transnational ties can be understood as occupying a continuum from low to high – that is, from very few and short-lived ties to those that are multiple and dense and continuous over time. For example, migrants may remit varying sums of money or none at all. This is also to say that, for our purposes, migrants and non-migrants should not be considered simply as transnational or not, but as being transnational to different degrees. Transnationality is characterized by transactions of varying degrees of intensity and at various stages of the life course; it is not restricted to geographical mobility. For example, non-mobile family members of migrants may engage in transnational practices.

To research transnationality has profound methodological implications. Since transnationalization can be observed to varying degrees in all spheres of social life, the 'container' of the nation-state cannot be taken as the sole and unquestioned unit of analysis or reference. Therefore, a focus on transnational social spaces and transnationality fits with scholarship which has addressed the questions of methodological nationalism (Wimmer and Glick Schiller 2003). Methodological nationalism needs to be unbundled into territorialism and essentialism.

First, transnational approaches aim to overcome territorialism – that is, conflating society, state and territory. Such territorialism is evident in many analyses which prioritize the state in the Weberian trilogy of the congruence of territory, authority and people. Many studies of migrant political participation take the container space of the nation-state as the singular frame of reference. Particularly pertinent is the fact that empirical data are collected and analysed largely on a nation-state basis and compared internationally. National state comparative work abounds in fields such as migration and immigration studies (for examples on both national state and transnational perspectives, see Martiniello and Rath 2010). If cross-border transactions are more important than this work leads us to believe, we need to open up the container. Second, transnational approaches also strive to overcome essentialism – that is, the conflation of society, state and nation. The problem to be addressed is the reification of important categories of national state thinking, such as nations and ethnicity. Even nowadays, transnational studies abound which look at particular national groups around the world and their relations to home countries instead of inquiring into how such groups are socially constituted and sustained in the first place. After all, it is worth noting that migrant networks or organizations can be built around various categorical distinctions, such as ethnicity, race, gender, schooling, professional training, political affiliation and sexual preference. It is far from clear that specific categories such as migrants always congeal around ethnic or national communities.

Aim and structure of the book

Cross-border or transnational migration is an ideal site to study how processes of transnationalization matter for the life courses of individuals and for the activities of groups and organizations. At the same time, the transnational perspective enables us to see how agents, migrants and non-migrants alike, are shaped and, in turn, actively shape their own destinies in a world in which cross-border transactions matter for life chances. Thus, we hold that not only do cross-border transformations impact upon agents, but also agents engage in transformative practices, and these importantly include cross-border transactions. It is this duality that underlies the analyses presented in this book. The chapters that follow deal with the main questions and challenges deriving from the realization of migrants' transnationality embedded in larger processes of transnationalization in all spheres of life, intertwined with the formation of transnational social spaces and their significance for crucial issues in the public sphere, such as economic development, social integration and citizenship.

Against this background, the objectives of the book are threefold. First, we seek to give an overview of transnationality by looking at cross-border ties and practices (chapter 2) and introduce the concept of transnational social spaces (chapter 3). Second, we show the significance of such a perspective for understanding migration and its consequences. Towards that end we discuss in more detail three substantive fields – development (chapter 4), migrant integration (chapter 5) and political practices (chapter 6) – which are crucial for understanding the life chances of migrants and non-migrants more generally. In the field of migration and development a transnational lens allows us to recognize the importance of, for example, diaspora and other communities for social change and economic transformation in regions of origin. It is thus migrants as cross-border development actors which is central. With respect to the integration of migrants, a transnational approach extends the view of the state as national container to ask the question: integration into what and where? And regarding political practices, the transnational perspective contributes to understanding how national institutions such as citizenship jump scale and partly incorporate cross-border views, such as in dual citizenship. Third, the book develops a transnational research methodology (chapter 7) and draws conclusions for general social science concepts – in particular, civil society as a principle of social order (chapter 8). A focus on civil society is pertinent for drawing together the results of the previous chapters because practices in transnational social spaces can thus be related to principles of social order such as the market, the state and the family.

By way of introducing the chapters, a note on the empirical examples is in order. Quite often these are drawn from a diverse range of situations, but more often than not from cases of cross-border migration concerning the United States and Mexico and the countries of Latin America and cases involving Turkey and Germany. First, these cases are prominent examples of what is called South–North migration and allow for an analysis of more than a hundred years and fifty years respectively of migration flows. Nonetheless, although the contexts differ widely – for example, the history prior to migration, the social conditions in the countries of both immigration and emigration, and the political regulation of migration and access to rights and citizenship – the basic tenets of transnationalization can be well described. Second, most examples refer to binational cross-border transactions only. Needless to say, we are aware that the web of ties maintained by migrants and their significant others often span several states. Take, for example, the associations of Alevis from Turkey, which spread across virtually all Nordic European countries as well as Germany, with significant transactions between organizations in the respective countries. However, the research undertaken thus far, perhaps for reasons of limited time and financial resources, has very rarely gone beyond a binational focus. It is a formidable challenge for future research, calling for truly transnational research teams (see chapter 7).

In order to account for the kinds of migrant practices that are prevalent in the familial, socio-cultural, economic and political spheres of social life, chapter 2 provides an overview. Certainly, such practices have been enhanced by faster and more intense communication channels across borders. Just as the declining cost of postage hastened the flow of letters back and forth over the Atlantic more than a century and a half ago, cheap telephone calls have been described as 'the social glue of migrant transnationalism' (Vertovec 2004). Two points are clarified. First, the chapter identifies the various kinds of social practices across borders in the familial, socio-cultural, economic and political spheres of social life. Second, it assesses the extent of these practices, thus locating them on the continuum of transnationality. For example, we know that family responsibilities do not entirely cease after some family members migrate. Therefore, we need to explore transnational kinship. It is necessary to clarify how caring from a distance – child-rearing through transnational motherhood or fatherhood and care of older persons in transnational settings – is organized. The transmission of a wide array of social and cultural ideas and practices, including views on gender and political ideas, is well documented. We also find manifold engagements of migrants in the economic realm. Prominent among these is transnational entrepreneurship, though remittances from migrants also play an important role. Finally, in the political realm there is, for example, the long-distance nationalist engagement of Tamils, Kurds and Palestinians but also other forms of engagement, such as migrant philanthropy or involvement in electoral politics through the use of voting rights by non-resident citizens.

Such practices concatenate into and take place in transnational social spaces (chapter 3). In essence, such spaces are populated by kinship groups, associations, networks of persons and organizations or communities that are located in between the micro-dynamics of personal ties and the macro-dynamics of large-scale social formations. The idea of transnational spaces entails considering migration as a border-breaking process in which two or more nation-states are penetrated by and become a part of a singular new social space. This social space involves the circulation of ideas, symbols, activities and material culture. Social space refers not only to physical features but also to larger opportunity structures, such as liberties in the respective political systems or property rights. In addition, the social life and the subjective images, values and meanings that the specific and limited place represents to migrants matter for the understanding of transnational social spaces. We use the concept of transnational social space above all as a heuristic tool to look at emerging social structures which have a dynamic of their own.

The following chapters focus on three substantive areas which constitute strategic research sites – migration and development, migrant integration, and political practices. Migration and development (chapter 4) is of utmost importance because it connects regions of origin, regions of destination and regions of onward migration through the idea of migrants as agents of development. The overwhelming majority of migration research focuses on countries of immigration, while the regions of origin play a peripheral role. They usually register either in accounts that explain why people migrate or in a one-sided focus on how economically backward regions – countries of emigration – can catch up with (post-)industrial economies. A transnational lens, however, establishes that the issue of cross-border migration and development is far from being an issue concerning mainly countries of emigration. Above all, migrants living outside the regions of origin at times play a crucial role, as evidenced by the recent efforts of international organizations and national governments in wooing diasporas and transnationally active migrant associations to play an active role in development policy. In the views of the World Bank and other international organizations, remittances have become the 'new development mantra' (Kapur 2004) as an effective means of reducing poverty and as a form of self-help. It is worth noting that financial remittances increased steadily from the early 1990s until 2008, when they decreased somewhat as a result of the global economic recession (figure 1.1). Whether the monies harvested by migration yield positive or negative development effects is, however, a question to which research provides no firm answer. Also, as noted in a report on migration issued by the United Nations Development Programme, 'remittances alone cannot remove the structural constraints to economic growth' (UNDP 2009: 79). Against this backdrop, the chapter discusses exchanges between migrants and stay-at-homes that can also yield the transmission of ideas, norms, expectations, skills and contacts acquired in the society of destination.

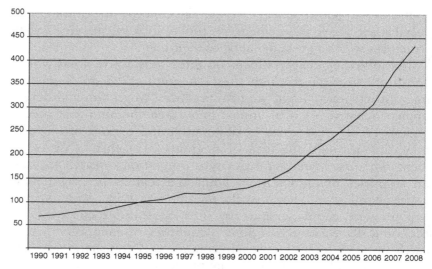

Figure 1.1 World remittance inflows (US$ million)

Source: World Bank (2008).

The second strategic research site – migrant integration (chapter 5) – is a classic in any account of migration and is usually discussed exclusively in terms of countries of immigration. By contrast, a transnational perspective pays attention to the fact that migrants also entertain meaningful ties with others abroad, raising the question of the entity into which migrants may socially integrate. Indeed, there may be several simultaneously: immigration and emigration, local and national and even a transnational scale, as in diasporas. This chapter offers an overview of the discussions which emerged around migrants' transnationality and theories of assimilation and ethnic pluralism: Is transnationalization and subsequent transnationality of migrants the end of classical assimilation, the melting of newcomers into an existing society or achieving equality with the members of dominant society? Is it an alternative to assimilation and therefore a new model of migrants' incorporation? The relationship of transnationalization and transnationality to assimilation was at the foundation of the 'transnationalism from below' discussion in the early 1990s. Interestingly, a transnational perspective entered the lexicon of migration studies at the time – more than a century after earlier generations of migration researchers had introduced and made extensive use of the concepts of assimilation and, to a lesser extent, cultural pluralism. It did so in rather different circumstances for, whereas assimilation and, partly, cultural pluralism gained currency at a time when migration research was in its early formative period, the transnational approach entered a well-developed sociological subfield dealing with migrant integration.

One of the claims was that the concept of assimilation did not live up to the task of describing the lived realities of cross-border migrants and that the transnational approach would do so. From this original transnational perspective developed in the early 1990s, not only assimilation but also cultural pluralism failed to account for new forms of incorporation. Whereas assimilation implies the loss of past identity, multiculturalism allegedly advances an essentialist perspective that treats ethnic identities as immutable (Basch et al. 1994). The new concept was not without its critics, however. The result is that the transnational approach has undergone substantial revision since its earliest formulations. Assimilation and cultural pluralism, on the one hand, and the cross-border expansion of social space, on the other, refer to different images: metaphorically, assimilation is associated with the image of 'the uprooted' (Handlin [1951] 1973) and cultural pluralism with 'the transplanted' (Bodnar 1985). An appropriate transnational metaphorical alternative – borrowing from the novelist Salman Rushdie – may be the idea of what we would call translated people – that is, migrants are continually engaged in translating languages, cultures, norms and social and symbolic ties: 'Having been borne across the world, we are translated men. It is normally supposed that something always gets lost in translation; I cling, obstinately, to the notion that something can also be gained' (Rushdie 1991: 16). Migrants do not forge their sense of identity and their community out of loss or mere replication.

The debate on the relationship between assimilation and transnationality has emerged in two stages. First, the two approaches were seen as mutually exclusive, each constituting a distinct model of migrant integration. Second, more recently, some thinkers have pointed towards a compatibility of assimilation and transnationality. According to this view, assimilation refers to a mode of immigrant integration into a receiving society, while transnationality is a mode of connectedness between and across the borders of various states. Thus, the two concepts refer to different processes, and the interesting question is: How do these two processes relate to each other?

The third strategic research site is political institutions and political practices (chapter 6). The focus of this chapter is on full membership in a national community – that is, citizenship. It is therefore especially important to see to what extent transnational ties have changed the practice and understanding of national citizenship and, vice versa, how political institutions and state policies shape political practices across borders. One prominent expression of how states respond to the transnationality of migrants is the increasing toleration of dual citizenship. The proportion of states around the world that allow dual citizenship rose from fewer than 5 per cent in 1959 to about 50 per cent in 2005, and the number is increasing (Faist 2010a). Dual citizenship arises when persons who acquire citizenship in a new country are allowed to keep their original citizenship or when children of binational parents are allowed to inherit the (different) citizenships of both. Such individuals then have two or more passports and, in principle, have access to rights as well as obligations in more than one polity. This raises the following questions: Do dual citizens have two votes, and does this therefore violate the principle of 'one person, one vote'? How relevant is the loyalty of dual citizens in times of war in the contemporary period? Is dual citizenship a sort of transnational citizenship independent of national citizenship?

Given the usefulness of a transnational perspective for substantive spheres of social life and crucial policy areas such as development, integration and citizenship, the question is which methodology is most appropriate (chapter 7). Such considerations have to reconcile talk of borderlessness with the continuing salience of national state borders. We therefore offer ways to overcome thinking in terms solely of the nation-state. Various methods are already available, including multi-sited fieldwork, the extended case method, global ethnography and network analysis, as well as quantitative surveys and longitudinal studies. In particular, the chapter gives examples of studies which strive to overcome three interconnected problems. First, there is the challenge of overcoming methodological nationalism – that is, the assumption of a congruence of societal practices and nation-states and the collection of data exclusively within the confines of the latter. Second, many transnational studies are still mired in essentialism by using exclusively ethnic or national groups as their starting point, which results in reifying characteristics of groups and thereby occluding other potentially relevant markers of heterogeneity, such as transnationality, but also class, gender, age or religion. Third, a transnational approach, which delves into systematic empirical analysis of sites in various states, often requires transnational research teams.

The concluding chapter synthesizes the previous insights and asks what they mean for our understanding of migration and other cross-border phenomena in the frames of civil society (chapter 8). First, civil society as a principle of social order connects closely to three additional principles of social order, namely the market, the state and the family. It thus brings in non-state, non-market and non-family principles of order and change. In particular, looking at transnational aspects of civil society raises questions about the forces conducive to the spread of democracy, human rights and the public sphere. In a nutshell, it is about all the 'good things' in societies. Yet civil society is Janus-faced, harbouring, for example, both long-distance nationalism and social movements pushing for democratization. Second, based on the methodological insights gained, we do not speak of transnational or global civil society (Keane 2003), as if what is conceived of as national civil society could and should be replicated on a global level. A transnational perspective does not try to imagine national state principles transnationally or globally in a linear fashion but looks at the constitution and the consequences of ties and practices across borders. This means that civil society as a principle of social order can be found neither exclusively at the national level nor solely at the transnational or global level. Instead, all scales on which civil society can be found to operate – local, national and beyond – have to be taken into account. Finally, this chapter closes with reflections of what a transnational perspective on cross-border migration and its consequences has to offer for a transnational turn in the social sciences more generally. This book provides a piece of the puzzle to unpack social practices towards more adequate understandings of society unbound.

2

Transnationality and Social Practices

Migrants engage in transnational social practices by travelling back and forth, through long-distance communication and by transferring financial and social remittances, among other means. From a transnational perspective it is crucial not only to focus on migrants in the country of immigration but to consider both sides of the migration process and the connections between 'here' and 'there'. This alerts us to the fact that migrants and relatively immobile residents in both countries engage in transnational practices and live in transnational social spaces (Faist 2000a). For instance, within transnational families, migrants organize long-distance parenting when their children are left behind, while children send emails to their parents. Migrants who send remittances back home to their families and international students who receive money for tuition fees from their parents constitute other examples (Khadria 2009: 109), indicating that cross-border flows do not go in one direction only but operate in both ways. Thus, transnational processes affect both migrants and non-migrants. 'Non-migrants who engage in core transnational practices are those whose social and economic lives depend upon and are shaped on a regular basis by resources, people, and ideas in the receiving-country context' (Levitt 2001b: 199). Thus, while classical approaches in migration research focus predominantly on migrants in the country of immigration, a transnational approach also takes into account non-migrants left behind in the country of emigration and the flows between the two. In taking into consideration cross-border activities of migrants and relatively immobile residents in both countries, a transnational framework for the study of migration has consequences for the ways in which empirical research is conducted (see chapter 7).

Migrants and non-migrants may engage in transnational practices in all spheres of social life (Levitt 2001b: 197; Itzigsohn and Saucedo 2002: 768). Nevertheless, for analytical purposes, transnational practices are often categorized with regard to different spheres. Along these lines a vast body of work in migration research addresses transnational practices in one or various spheres of society (see, among others, Levitt and Jaworsky 2007; Vertovec 2009). The rest of this chapter gives an overview of transnational practices in four basic spheres of transnational life: the familial, socio-cultural, economic and political. All of these are illustrated by typical examples from interviews conducted in the German survey Transnationalization, Migration and Transformation: Multi-Level Analysis of Migrant Transnationalism (TRANS-NET).[3] Based on the case studies, some characteristics of the corresponding sphere of social life are emphasized. The chapter closes with a discussion on the significance of transnational practices by giving insights into their extent and intensity. Here transnationality is understood as ranging along a continuum from low to high.

Familial transnational practices

Case study 2.1 Emre

Emre was born in 1971 in Turkey. When he was a small child his parents moved to Germany as guest workers, as did many Turkish migrants in the 1960s and 1970s who wanted to improve their economic situation. Emre was left in the care of his grandparents in Turkey.

> I believe it was after I was one year old that my parents came to Germany as guest workers, first my mother and after six months

also my father. That meant for me that there was no mother after my first year of life. And I grew up with my maternal grandparents. It was only later, sometime between the ages of four or five, that I realized that my natural parents were not who I thought they were and that they were in Germany, and at the same time I realized that I had a brother who was four year younger than I am. Probably because of their fear of losing me completely, and also due to their love and desire for me, my parents made an attempt to integrate me in Germany when I was five years old. This didn't go very well, since my parents were in employment and worked shifts. And I also had difficulties getting used to Germany . . . and to my parents and to my brother. This is why at the age of six I went back to my grandparents again, and there I also went to primary school. Yes, that went well for two years. Then my parents decided in 1979 to bring me to Germany permanently. Yes, since 1979 I have been in Germany.

Now, as an adult, Emre travels once a year to Turkey for holidays and, unlike his three brothers, who were born in Germany, he still has contact with his relatives there. The relationship with his grandmother, under whose care he grew up, is especially important.

Usually, I fly to Turkey once a year when nothing intervenes . . . And of course I still maintain very good contacts with my relatives in Turkey . . . I've contact with my maternal grandmother, whom I've seen as father and mother. This relationship is still very intimate, and my grandmother is still alive and was here [in Germany] this winter. And I still got to know her and she is already very old – well, unfortunately it soon could come to an end.

As in the case of Emre's parents, who moved to Germany as guest workers to earn money, migration can be seen as one of several strategies of upward social mobility, pursued in order to reduce family risks and ensure the core or even extended family a better life. Migration processes are not based exclusively on individual decisions but rather must be understood in the context of family strategies (Stark 1991: 39). Sending family members abroad may be an investment for the livelihood of the whole family. Thus, spatial dispersal as migration strategy is 'often a rational family decision to preserve the family, a resourceful and resilient way of strengthening it: families split in order to be together trans-locally' (Chan 1997: 195). Accordingly, families do not necessarily migrate together. In the case of labour migrants who search for employment in other countries, the movement of families is often restricted or even excluded by stringent immigration policy. In the course of war, migrants may also be displaced from their families, as illustrated in the case of refugees from Bosnia-Herzegovina (Al-Ali 2002). In these circumstances migrants and refugees work and reside in the country of immigration while leaving their families behind. Different forms of separation may thus occur, such as of (married) partners, parents from their children, children from their siblings, and grandparents from their grandchildren. The result is that migrants and their family members are located in places in at least two distinct nation-states.

In some cases many years may pass before the family is reunited, as migrants continue to live and work in the country of immigration and conditions for family members to join them are limited. However, this does not necessarily lead to broken families. Rather, families separated by migration have to organize their lives spanning national borders. Thus, transnationality becomes a characteristic of individuals and families as a whole. '"Transnational families" are defined here as families that live some or most of the time separated from each other, yet hold together and create something that can be seen as a feeling of collective welfare and unity, namely "familyhood", even across national borders' (Bryceson and Vuorela 2002: 3). Studies of cross-border family practices point out that the family does not necessarily require unilocal residence. Nevertheless, changes and transformations within nuclear and extended families are observable after they are maintained across borders. 'In the migration process, the family undergoes changes because it must continue to meet the same set of needs within a dramatically changed context' (Landolt and Da 2005: 627). Transnationality in the private sphere can be attributed to the fact that responsibilities and obligations do not cease when migrants move to another country, leaving their family members back home. Rather, migrants have to organize simultaneously their daily work lives in one country and their private family lives in another. Even when it is not possible to share in the daily life of their families, migrants continue to perform caring roles and to meet the material and emotional needs of family members. Long-distance family practices performed by migrants include care of both children and the elderly.

As mentioned previously, migration may lead to a separation of parents and children. Many of the parents who migrate to take advantage of better labour market opportunities leave their children behind. In these cases it is mostly close relatives – usually the other parent, the grandmother, or other female kin – but also paid caregivers who provide for the children's daily needs. But even though parents who have migrated to another country may not be able to provide care on a daily and face-to-face basis, they are not released from their responsibilities. Women in particular are faced with the challenge of providing childcare over long distances, as illustrated by studies on 'transnational motherhood' (Hondagneu-Sotelo and Avila 1997: 554) and 'female-headed transnational families' (Parreñas 2001a: 361). Female migrants must often fulfil familial obligations in the country of immigration by earning money and simultaneously act as caregivers in a transnational setting. As a Latina migrant in the United States put it, 'I'm here, but I'm there' (Hondagneu-Sotelo and Avila 1997: 558). These conditions not only create logistic complications for female migrants but also result in emotional costs for parents and children (Parreñas 2001a: 386; Mazzucato and Schans 2011). For example, Emre perceived his grandparents to be his parents, since they took care of him, and when he was reunited with his natural parents and his younger brother in Germany he initially felt the situation to be unfamiliar.

Moreover, the case of Emre's grandmother indicates that not only children but also elderly parents and grandparents are left behind by migrants. If they too are in need of care, this kind of support across generations is also affected by geographical distance. It becomes apparent that face-to-face interactions or physical contacts are often an indispensable requirement for caregiving, which demands continuous or frequent effort, time and presence (Zechner 2008: 37). Thus, migrants often find it impossible to fulfil the role expected of them as carers of those elderly parents and grandparents left behind.

Socio-cultural transnational practices

Case study 2.2   Kamber

After undertaking voluntary work for various organizations in the areas of migration and integration in Germany, Kamber became the manager of a German–Turkish association. Most of the association's interests are related to the cultural sphere. It has manifold relationships with Turkey and, thus, Kamber's activities often involve dealing with people and organizations there.

> As manager of the house, I actually have to deal with Turkey almost every day, particularly with ministries and cultural organizations in Turkey. We work closely with foundations in the areas of the arts and culture in Istanbul. We deal with artists in Turkey all the time, whom we invite to events. Also, managers, record companies, whatever – you name it. In all kinds of areas.

Moreover, the child of binational parents who had met when his mother was on holiday in Turkey, Kamber has dual citizenship and speaks both German and Turkish fluently. He is of the opinion that all migrants and their descendants should be allowed to hold dual citizenship. For him this best corresponds to his own identity.

> Personally I've the situation that I'm German and Turk and thus it is actually logical for me that I've both citizenships . . . For me actually there was never a question of choosing between am I

> Turk now and am I German now, but I was always both in some sense. I've German behaviours, I've Turkish behaviours. And sometimes I think Turkish, sometimes I talk German.

As in the case of Kamber, socio-cultural transnational practices may be characterized by a certain degree of institutionalization. Here, the artistic and cultural exchanges take place in the framework of a German–Turkish association based in Germany. Other more institutionalized transnational practices going beyond private life include the participation in hometown associations or in charity organizations linked to the country of emigration (Itzigsohn and Saucedo 2002: 777). Even if these are rather different sets of transnational practices, they are all undertaken within the broad spectrum of migration-related organizations and associations that are socio-cultural in nature. Moreover, they have in common that they build community relations across national borders. 'Sociocultural transnationalism refers to those transnational linkages that involve the recreation of a sense of community that encompasses migrants and people in the place of origin' (ibid.: 768).

However, transnational socio-cultural practices are not necessarily based on any stable, ongoing migrant-based organizations or collective initiatives, as in the case of Kamber, but can also be performed by ad hoc groups aimed at specific projects. They include, as shown for Colombia, 'cases in which immigrants had informally gathered voluntary monetary and non-monetary contributions to meet some specific local need in their locality of origin, such as providing scholarships for the poor, building a classroom, contributing equipment to hospitals and other public facilities, or donating fire trucks, ambulances, and so forth' (Guarnizo and Díaz 1999: 412–13). Both kinds of practices, carried out by stable organizations or more informally, and undertaken by quite different migration flows, such as old resident returnees, new working-class emigrants and migrants connected to the drug trade, may converge in a dense web of transnational relations linking migrants and their places of origin, as illustrated by the field research in Colombia by Guarnizo and Díaz.

Regardless of whether stable organizations and associations or more informal practices are taken into account, these various examples open up a view beyond monetary remittances, which are at the centre in migration research, and illustrate that social and cultural ideas and practices are also transmitted and received in transnational settings. These migration-driven forms of cultural diffusion can be summarized under the term 'social remittances': 'Social remittances are the ideas, behaviors, identities, and social capital that flow from receiving- to sending-country communities' (Levitt 1998: 927). They are transferred by migrants when they interact with the country of immigration. At least three types of social remittances can be distinguished (ibid.: 933–6; see also Levitt 2001a: 59–63). The first type is 'normative structures' and involves the exchange of ideas, values and beliefs. Taking the example of gender, it is shown that, on their return, female Bangladeshi labour migrants to Malaysia brought back new norms of gender equality – in particular, that Muslim women could engage in work outside the household. This was made possible, among other things, by the fact that Malaysia, a successful Islamic country, is regarded as trendsetter in terms of female employment outside the home (Dannecker 2005). The second type is 'systems of practices', which are made up of actions shaped by normative structures. In the case of Bangladeshi migrant women, this means that the observation of new versions of gender ideologies in Malaysia led to transformations of existing gender relations in Bangladesh. Female migrants have introduced new gender practices following their return, and non-migrant women adopted some of these practices. The third type of social remittance is 'social capital', since the social capital acquired by migrants in the country of immigration may be transferable to the country of origin. With regard to gender, for instance, migrant women may make use of the gendered social capital accrued within their social networks in the country of immigration to help family members back home – for example, by enabling them to access resources such as health care. And even if, in the case of female Bangladeshi migrants, in contrast to their male counterparts, their social position and status had decreased with their migration, after their return they were able to give loans to other women who planned to migrate and thereby established a new credit system in Bangladesh. Social remittances may involve not only gender ideologies and gendered social capital but also political ideas such as concepts of human rights and democracy, among other things (Faist 2008: 34). It is important to mention, however, that the transfer of social remittances by migrants and non-migrants does not reveal anything about how they are used. Moreover, social remittances can have positive as well as negative effects (see also chapter 4).

Another important aspect with regard to the socio-cultural dimension of transnationalization is the issue of personal identity. Identities may also be affected by transnational processes, as the case of Kamber illustrates. Kamber's identity is not characterized by a sense of belonging to only one nation-state; rather, he created a dual mode of belonging. This example shows that contemporary migrants and their descendants do not necessarily lose their past identity when living in the country of immigration but may form fluid and multiple identities. Transnational studies emphasize the need to take into consideration not only concrete activities but also more symbolic and subjective dimensions of transnationality. Accordingly, transnational approaches started to take into account both social and symbolic ties (Faist 1998: 218), objective and subjective dimensions of transnational practices (Levitt et al. 2003: 571), or ways of being and ways of belonging (Levitt and Glick Schiller 2004: 1010–11).

Economic transnational practices

Case study 2.3   Özlem

In 1971, Özlem, a Turkish citizen who is now aged fifty-five, immigrated to Germany, where she married her German husband. During the initial period in Germany Özlem received financial remittances from her family in Turkey.

They have given me support ... Yes, for example, first of all when I was married, my husband was a student. Yes, he was a student and then I was a young mother, one could say. Yes, we needed everything. For example, they paid for our holidays and put money in our pocket and dressed us in new clothes there [in Turkey] ... It was like that until we earned money ourselves.

Throughout her life Özlem has been self-employed in various lines of business. She currently sells evening and wedding dresses to customers of Turkish immigrant origin in Germany. The clothes are made at factories run by family members in Turkey and at other Turkish companies. Özlem and her new partner have numerous business contacts in Turkey, such as her stepfather.

Therefore I've my stepfather there [in Turkey] and he brings the cheques there ... One enlists all people. Or he has two people or also my partner has his people, and we say, 'Can you quickly go to the airport, someone brings samples. Can you quickly go to the airport, you have to send that', that's how it works. One has to – and we've enough people.

Özlem communicates mainly via telephone and email, but she also occasionally travels to Turkey, thereby always trying to combine her professional and private life.

I go there [to Turkey] for business for ten days and then try to stay for the weekend, so I can see my daughter. I have just opened my own fashion studio in another [Turkish] city, and when I go there I can only see my daughter for two hours during the stopover at the airport.

The globalization of capital and labour creates not only needs but also new opportunities for economic practices among migrants. Migration itself is often driven by economic considerations, especially when migrants move to another country in search of employment. Moreover, migrants and non-migrants undertake a vast variety of transnational economic practices. The spectrum ranges from small-scale and informal practices, such as sending remittances, to larger-scale and more formal practices, such as transnational entrepreneurship, both visible in the case of Özlem.

Financial remittances (see also chapters 1 and 4) constitute one form of transnational economic practice directly involving migrants and include two-way flows between the countries of emigration and immigration (Mazzucato 2006; Faist 2010b: 78). At least three different types of economic remittances can be distinguished (Guarnizo 2003: 671–80; Goldring 2004: 812–32). First, the largest share of financial remittances is used as income. Money is sent abroad to support children or spouses but also to help other relatives or friends. Remittances are often sent in particular on the basis of kin solidarity and reciprocal obligation. Being a member of a family or a community often goes along with responsibilities to help that family or social network to survive. Monetary remittances intended to maintain and improve the standard of living of the family or household are used for recurrent expenses, such as food, housing and clothing, but also for education and health services. Such remittances end in cases of family reunification in the country of immigration or return migration or if relatives living abroad have also emigrated or died. A second type of remittance is entrepreneurial, where monetary remittances are used for building houses or for the acquisition of land, but also for establishing small businesses. In contrast to familial remittances, this type is primarily investment oriented and may be used either to establish a new business or to investment in existing businesses. A third type of monetary remittance comprises funds used by individual immigrants or hometown associations to finance community projects in the country of emigration. These projects are related to basic infrastructure, such as building roads, or public services for education, health and social security, but also for recreation, such as sports fields. Such remittances are thus meant to support local community development (see also chapter 4). The community projects may involve government actors and institutions, as for example in the case of Mexico (Guarnizo 2003: 674; Goldring 2004: 830).

With regard to the situation between Turkey and Germany (Faist 1998; 2000a: 214–18), financial remittances, and especially familial remittances, were relevant primarily in the early 1960s until the 1970s and 1980s. Most of these remittances were transferred by labour migrants and return migrants or invested in housing and consumer products in Turkey. Such remittances decreased slightly in the 1980s and 1990s, probably as a result of family reunification. More recently they have been replaced by entrepreneurship as the now dominant economic practice undertaken by Turkish migrants. Thus, the period from 1983 to 1992 was characterized by the growing importance of ethnic enterprises established by Turkish immigrants, and the number of self-employed Turks tripled, from about 10,000 to 35,000. The enterprises were located in a variety of economic sectors and included among others grocery shops, craft works, travel agencies and restaurants. Many of the enterprises established by Turkish migrants relied on the work of family members. However, during this period entrepreneurial practices among migrants were limited to the local markets in Germany. Only later did they move from ethnic niche businesses to become transnational. While not the case for the majority, a proportion of Turkish migrants entered fields in which they found themselves competing with German businesses. Moreover, existing and newly established contacts with Turkey enabled migrants to operate transnationally. In textile production especially, transnational entrepreneurs such as Özlem could take advantage of the much lower costs in Turkey and thus moved production there. At the same time, they retained their sales and distribution centres in Germany.

In sum, transnational entrepreneurs can be conceptualized as company owners and the self-employed who travel abroad for business and whose success of their enterprise depends on regular contacts with foreign countries, especially with their country of origin (Portes et al. 2002: 284). For example, transnational entrepreneurship is based on a whole range of exchange of goods, capital, services and labour forces across at least two countries. Five types of transnational entrepreneurial practice can be distinguished (Zhou 2004: 1055):

- financial services, such as informal remittances handling agencies
- import and export – for example, of evening and wedding dresses (as in the case of Özlem)
- cultural enterprises which, among others, trade music and movies or organize musical, dancing or sports teams
- manufacturing firms, such as garment factories
- return migrant micro-enterprises, including restaurants and car sales and service.

All in all, contemporary migrants are not only involved in small business ownership, such as fast-food restaurants, newsstands or nail salons, but also now engage in entrepreneurial practices that 'have become increasingly heterogeneous in scale, range, intensity, and levels of formality or institutionalisation' (ibid.: 1065–6).

Political transnational practices

Case study 2.4   Adnan

When he was less than a year old, the Turkish-born Adnan migrated to Germany, where his father had an attractive job offer. Throughout his childhood he maintained contact with his extended family in Turkey. After studies and work experiences abroad, among others in Turkey, he has been back in Germany for three years and now works for a government agency. His professional activities give him 'the opportunity to help shape the integration policy'. Adnan's 'migration background' was not an obstacle to finding employment; it actually helped him get his current job, enabling him to facilitate understanding and dialogue between Turkish migrant organizations and the Turkish community in Germany, on the one hand, and German political and administrative institutions, on the other: 'In particular, persons with a Turkish background who play a bridging role do both; they help the

[German] government to understand the Turkish position, but they also affect the Turkish community.'

In addition to participating in the German political system, Adnan is also concerned with Turkish politics. As an employee of a German government agency, he often works with Turkish political organizations and institutions.

> Professional contacts [in Turkey] have increased since I returned [to Germany] and started to work for the government. I'm engaged in integration politics, and there are a lot of issues that can only be resolved with the help of Turkey. Since many Turks living in Germany continue to be Turkish citizens, my professional contact to Turkey has been very intensive over the last three years.

In Adnan's case, political transnational practices are based solely on his employment in a German government agency. Thus, he participates indirectly in the country of his parents via an institution located in Germany. Indirect political participation by migrants and their descendants in the country of emigration can be distinguished from various forms of direct cross-border participation (Østergaard-Nielsen 2003a: 762; 2003b: 22). These direct forms include, among other things, voting in elections in the country of origin, support to political parties and campaigns abroad, participation in hometown associations, membership in political associations active in the country of emigration, and political media consumption. All in all, migrants and their descendants can be involved in different forms of political transnationalization, participating either directly or indirectly.

Such forms of political transnationality illustrate that transnational research needs to go beyond two shortcomings of the predominant research on political activities undertaken by migrants. On the one hand, the focus of research into the political practices of immigrants in Europe is generally on participation in the country of settlement (Østergaard-Nielsen 2003a: 764; 2003b: 6). These studies look at the inclusion of migrants in the political system and their integration in the society of the country of immigration. From this perspective, transnational practices, if considered at all, are seen mainly as an obstacle to successful political and social integration. On the other hand, in studies on political transnationality the focus is generally on the emigrants' political participation in the country of emigration (Bauböck 2003: 700). These studies investigate how migrants are embedded in the political landscape of their country of origin. Different from both approaches, contemporary transnational research turns away from analysing simply one or the other towards a more comprehensive picture of transnational political practices.

Immigrant politics and homeland politics can thus be differentiated as two basic dimensions of migrants' transnational practices (Østergaard-Nielsen 2003a: 762–3; 2003b: 21). Immigrant politics are aimed at improving the situation of migrants in the new country, including, for example, practices geared to obtaining more rights. Adnan's professional activities, for example, are directed precisely towards such objectives. But his case also demonstrates that, for the achievement of these integration-related objectives, cross-border collaboration with political organizations and institutions located in Turkey are helpful. Here, the emigration country becomes involved in supporting its nationals in the immigration country. This shows that practices related to immigrant politics can also have a transnational dimension. Homeland politics, on the other hand, pertains to the domestic or foreign policy of the homeland. Migrants' political orientation towards their country of origin can involve both opposition and support. Homeland politics can be further differentiated into emigrant politics, diaspora politics and translocal politics. The subset of emigrant politics is related to all issues of migrants' legal, economic and political status in the emigration country – for example, the demands for external voting rights and tax exemptions. Diaspora politics relates to migrant collectives who engage in homeland nation-building projects (for more detail, see chapter 6). Finally, translocal politics consists of initiatives undertaken by migrants to improve the situation in the local community of their country of origin, including the support of development projects.

All in all, the dimensions of migrants' transnational political practices are not mutually exclusive. There is no zero-sum relationship between political practices in the country of immigration and that of emigration. Rather, as the example of Adnan illustrates, they can take place simultaneously and even complement each other.

Not only do migrants have an impact on politics in the countries of immigration and emigration, but their transnational practices depend on the situation in both countries. The context in the countries of immigration and the mobilizing role of the countries of emigration affect the process of political transnationalization among migrants (Østergaard-Nielsen 2001, 2003a, 2003b). Processes of transnationalization among migrants are related to political issues of equal rights, discrimination and citizenship in their new countries. Transnational political practices with regard to both domestic and foreign policies are not only driven by integration policies but are also a reaction to events and developments in the country of emigration. For example, the laws and policies of home countries are important in determining whether or not their nationals acquire the citizenship of their new country (Freeman and Ögelman 1998). Moreover, transnational political practices can also be based on homeland conflicts, as is the case in the Turkish–German context, where Kurdish organizations in Germany are engaged in supporting Kurds in Turkey (Faist 1998). The solidarity and material support flowing from activists in Germany to PKK warriors and those sympathetic to that organization intensified the armed conflict in Turkey. Kurds living in Germany demand more cultural and political autonomy for Kurds in the Republic of Turkey.

However, political transnationalization by migrants may comprise more than political activities across state borders. Migration becomes 'transnational . . . when it creates overlapping membership, rights and practices that reflect a simultaneous belonging of migrants to two different political communities' (Bauböck 2003: 705). For example, Kamber's dual citizenship, as shown in the case study, is accompanied by a sense of belonging to both countries. Thus, there is a need to focus not only on transnational political practices but also on multiple political memberships in terms of collective identities and citizenship. While transnational political activism in most cases is limited to the first generation of immigrants, a largely passive affiliation to the country of emigration is much more widespread and can persist also among their children (ibid.: 711).

The significance of transnational practices

Even though each of the selected case studies represents one specific sphere of social life, migrants and their children may participate simultaneously in various transnational practices. To capture the variable degree of transnational involvement in different spheres, a distinction between comprehensive and selective transnational practices can be drawn. 'Some individuals whose transnational practices involve many areas of social life engage in comprehensive transnational practices while others engage in transnational practices that are more selective in scope' (Levitt 2001b: 198–9; see also Levitt and Waters 2002: 11). An example of the former is Emre, who participates in familial, socio-cultural, economic and political processes. Besides maintaining relationships with his relatives in Turkey, he is the leader of a folk dance group which draws inspirations from traditional and modern dances in Turkey and buys its costumes there. Moreover, the group was founded mainly by left-wing intellectuals from the first generation of Turkish migrants in Germany, and the group is still interested in Turkish policies. An example of the latter would be Özlem, whose transnational practices are limited to the economic and familial spheres, both of which generally go hand in hand.

Alongside the scope of transnational practices across different spheres of social life, the question of how widespread transnational practices are among migrants has raised considerable scholarly debate. From this perspective, by generalizing it to the entire migrant population, the phenomenon of transnationalization was overestimated by the initial conceptualization of transnational theorizing. While most research on transnationality draws on case studies and participant observation to show evidence of transnational practices in the various contexts, such studies have not allowed for any conclusions as to their extent and intensity (Faist 2004a: 5; see also chapter 7). In the following it will be shown that, first, not all migrants are involved in transnational practices and, second, even those who are do so to different degrees.

Most of the efforts to investigate more precisely the extent of transnationality in different spheres of social life are based on the Comparative Immigrant Entrepreneurship Project (CIEP),[4] which was the first survey explicitly designed for this purpose. The overall result of the project shows that not all contemporary migrants ought to be seen as transnational migrants in a strong sense – that is, characterized by a high degree of transnationality (Portes 2001: 183; 2003: 876). The transnational practices of Colombian, Dominican and Salvadorian migrants in the United States are not very widespread across the economic, political and socio-cultural spheres of social life (Portes 2003). By focusing on the economic sphere, it was found that the proportion of respondents who participated in transnational entrepreneurial practices did not exceed 6 per cent of the sample. In the political sphere, both kinds of practices, electoral and non-electoral, were measured. While regular transnational participation did not exceed 10 per cent, occasional participation was more common, even if it did not exceed one-fifth of the sample. The results in the socio-cultural sphere, where the focus was on various forms of civic activities (see chapter 8), show that only one-third of the sample participated at least occasionally in transnational socio-cultural practices. However, even if the majority of the Latino immigrants considered in the CIEP survey does not maintain transnational practices on a regular basis, a sizeable minority becomes engaged in transnationalization at least occasionally. In sum, while mass migration generates an infrastructure facilitating cross-border practices, regular engagement is not characteristic of all migrants and their descendants.

As these findings already indicate, based on the CIEP, statements can be made on the intensity of transnational practices among migrants. In this respect, different degrees of transnational involvement became obvious. Accordingly, José Itzigsohn and his colleagues distinguish between 'narrow' and 'broad' forms of transnationality (Itzigsohn et al. 1999: 323; see also Itzigsohn and Saucedo 2002: 770). Narrow transnationality refers to continuous participation in transnational practices, while broad transnationality means only sporadic involvement. A similar distinction is that by Luis Guarnizo and his colleagues (cf. Levitt 2001b: 198; see also Guarnizo et al. 2003) between 'core' and 'expanded' transnationalism. Whereas the first term is related to regular transnational practices, the second refers to transnational practices on an occasional basis. Both approaches aim to point out different degrees of intensity, and so describe the variation by a binary distinction between deep involvement in transnationalization, on the one hand, and only sporadic or occasional participation, on the other. Going beyond such binary distinctions, we suggest that transnationality should be understood as a marker of heterogeneity and, thus, as ranging along a continuum from low to high (see chapter 1; see also Faist et al. 2011; Fauser and Reisenauer 2012). In cases of high degrees of transnationality, multiple and dense transnational practices may become condensed within transnational social spaces, as will be shown in chapter 3. All in all, the focus on the extent and intensity of transnational practices in this section clarifies that the analytical concept of transnationality has to be further refined to describe adequately the empirical phenomenon of cross-border practices undertaken by migrants.

3

Conceptualizing Transnationalization and Transnational Social Spaces

As illustrated in chapter 2, transnational practices among migrants and their home country counterparts are observable in various spheres of social life – the familial, the socio-cultural, the economic and the political. But it has also been shown that only a certain proportion of migrants engage in transnational social practices. And, for those who do, these practices can be differentiated with respect to intensity. In further specifying those migrants who undertake transnational practices, and their degree of involvement, current research goes beyond the initial conceptualization of transnationalism where all contemporary migrants were regarded as 'transmigrants' (Glick Schiller et al. 1992b). So also does the discussion about whether transnational life among migrants and non-migrants is a 'new' phenomenon that emerged only during migration processes in the late twentieth century or one that could also be found in earlier times. For a clarification of the contentious issue regarding past versus present transnationalization, the first section of this chapter consists of a historical perspective. A central aspect is the changing conditions of transnationalization. It is shown that, in particular, transformations in the technology of transportation and communication, as well as economic, political and cultural dynamics in the countries of immigration and emigration, are conducive to the emergence of transnational practices in the migration context. Second, the chapter presents transnational social spaces as key to characterizing condensed formations of transnational ties and practices. Transnational social spaces are introduced as a heuristic tool, and a systematic typology of their manifestations is presented. The development of the concept of transnational social spaces offers a unique opportunity to look into the formation of different types that span at least two nation-states. Third, this chapter not only addresses the newness of transnationalization and gives insights into the concept of transnational social spaces but also raises the question whether these are enduring or temporary phenomena. The durability of transnational social formations is discussed with regard to both life course and generation.

Transnationalization in historical perspective

Past and present transnationalization

Those scholars who initially embraced the idea of transnational ties maintained by migrants did so because of a conviction that it was necessary to capture the distinctive and characteristic features of the new immigration streams and groups that have emerged in the advanced industrialized countries at the core of the capitalist world system. The terms transnationalization, transnational social spaces and transnationality (see chapter 1) have emerged and evolved at a time characterized by high levels of labour migration from economically less developed countries to the most developed states, and of political refugees fleeing conflicts and instability in former communist and Third World countries. The influx of these new labour migrants and refugees has reshaped not only nation-states with long histories of immigration – the settler states of the United States, Canada and Australia – but also countries that have not been notable as immigrant receiving nations in the earlier phases of industrialization – those of Western Europe and, to a lesser extent, Japan. The high levels of immigration, the new locales of settlement, the reshaped ethnic, religious and linguistic mixes, the changes in the nature of capitalist economies in a new (post-)industrial epoch, the changes in the meaning and significance attached to the ideas of citizenship, and the potency of a globalized popular culture – these are factors that have all contributed to the conviction that what is novel about the present requires equally novel conceptual tools if we are to make sense of the impact of the new international migration on the countries of immigration, transition and emigration. Against this background, the earliest articulation of transnationalism in migration research by the anthropologist Nina Glick Schiller and her colleagues (1992b) introduced a conceptual framework for understanding contemporary international migration. These scholars suggested that here is a new type of migrant today compared with his or her late nineteenth- and early twentieth-century counterpart, and 'that transnational migration differs significantly from previous migration experience' (Glick Schiller et al. 1992a: x; for a critical assessment, see Kivisto 2001: 551–7).

Over the past decade there has been much debate about the similarities and differences between earlier and contemporary migrant transnationalization. In this context, scholars have questioned whether contemporary migrant transnationality is a new phenomenon (see, among others, Faist 2000a: 211; Levitt 2001a: 21–2; Portes 2003: 874–5). Nancy Foner (2001), in particular, makes the argument that transnational processes have a long history. She provides some insights into transnationalization past and present by comparing immigrants in New York City today with those at the turn of the twentieth century. For the earlier period she focuses on Eastern European Jews and Italians, and for contemporary migrants she considers immigrants from Asian, West Indian and Latin American nations and from European countries. For the earlier European immigrants Foner demonstrates that, while living in New York, they simultaneously maintained familial, cultural, economic and political links to their home societies. Just as with contemporary immigrants, the reasons for sustaining transnational relationships were, in particular, links to relatives left behind and sentiment towards home communities and countries. Russian Jews and Italians in early twentieth-century New York had already established what would later be termed by social scientists 'transnational households', and sent letters and remittances to relatives and friends in the countries of emigration. They were engaged in hometown associations or Jewish *landsman-shaftn* in New York, followed news of the emigration country, and remained involved in home-country politics. All in all, they lived transnational lives in ways similar to those of contemporary immigrants. This was especially true of those earlier immigrants who moved to New York temporarily with the intent of returning home – they actively maintained transnational linkages. A long-held practice among those migrants was to buy land or houses in their country. Many not only cherished the dream of eventually returning but also realized it. According to Foner, 'nationwide, return migration rates are actually lower now than they were in the past' (Foner 2001: 39). However, there are differences to be found between Russian Jews and Italians. Many of the former abandoned the idea of return after 1900 because of revolution-ary upheaval and the increasing intensity of pogroms in Russia. While Russian Jews thus tended to be permanent settlers, 'Italians were the quintessential transnational New Yorkers of their time, as much commuters as many contemporary immigrants' (ibid.: 40). Many of them stayed in New York seasonally or for some years before returning to Italy. But a large number of those who had returned also remigrated later. Overall, Italian migrants had a tendency to travel back and forth across the Atlantic. The motives for this movement were, among others, economic issues and the improved methods of transportation by the end of the nineteenth century, but also a lack of acceptance in America. In sum, Foner's study of past and present migration indicates that there is nothing essentially new in what is referred to as migrant transnationaliza-tion and transnationality, and that European immigrants in New York at the turn of the twentieth century can also be described in transnational terms.

Another scholar who brings a historical perspective to the ques-tion concerning the newness of transnational life does so with a focus exclusively on the family. Deborah Bryceson's work (2002) is based on a comparison of today's transnational families in Europe with families involved in mass migration from Europe to the US in the latter half of the nineteenth century. Concluding that transnational families are not a new phenomenon, she illustrates that transnational family formation involving migrants from Europe already took place before the latter half of the twentieth century. By contrasting family networking in the nineteenth and twentieth centuries, she addresses similarities and differences between families in past and present cross-border migration. As an example of a transnational family in past migration, she presents the Onninks, Dutch migrants to the US in 1865. By contrast, the Ouarrouds, Moroccan emigrants to the Netherlands in 1974, represent a present-day transnational family. Both families migrated at a major economic turning point in search of economic opportunities. But while the Onninks migrated as a couple just a day after their marriage, leaving behind their elderly parents and other relatives, the Ouarroud couple lived apart for several years. Moreover, while the Onninks retained a strong patriarchal tradition, the Ouarroud spouses eventually divorced and the family became female headed. Based on these two examples, Bryceson points out that the individuals who had migrated in both cases maintained transnational relationships with the families left behind and that, therefore, transnational families are nothing new. What certainly has changed are family roles with regard to gender and generations (Bryceson 2002: 56).

Conditions for present processes of transnationalization

The central argument offered by both Foner and Bryceson is that there are continuities between past and present transnationalization, with migrants from both periods actively participating in familial, socio-cultural, economic and political practices linking at least two countries. But, if the phenomenon of transnationalization is not new, the question emerges as to what is quantitatively or qualitatively different now in comparison with the past? Even if transnational practices can be documented for migrants in former times, transnational approaches argue that 'they lacked the elements of regularity, routine involvement, and critical mass characterizing contemporary examples of transnationalism. Few immigrants actually lived in two countries in terms of their routine daily activities' (Portes et al. 1999: 223–4). Transnationalization has expanded nowadays with respect to both the number of migrants and the intensity of their involvement in this kind of practice. One of the crucial factors identified by transnational approaches contributing to the rise of the phenomenon is transformations in the technology of transportation and communication (ibid.; Foner 2001: 42–4; Levitt 2001a: 22–4). The relevant technological breakthroughs occurred in the nineteenth century with the introduction of such new and improved methods of travel and communication as transoceanic steamship passage and telegraph communication. The ongoing transportation and communication revolution has considerably decreased the costs of bridging long geographical distances. This trend accelerated sharply after the Second World War and especially from the 1970s (Faist 1998: 223; 2000a: 212). Increased accessibility between the countries of immigration and emigration allowed transnational interconnections to be more frequent and dense. The availability of routine and inexpensive air travel makes physical movement faster and easier. Many migrants can fly home for annual vacations, to visit relatives and friends, or to take part in significant events such as weddings or elections. New and cheaper technologies enable rapid communication across national borders. In contrast to the past, contemporary migrants do not have to wait two weeks or even longer for a reply to a letter but can communicate immediately with their relatives and friends abroad by telephone or email (Foner 2001: 43–4; Levitt 2001a: 23–4). All in all, transformations in transportation and communication technologies permit easier, closer and more frequent interconnections between countries of immigration and emigration. They allow immigrants to be actively involved in the everyday lives of their home country counterparts.

Even if technological breakthroughs make cross-border practices among migrants and non-migrants easier and more common, there remain variations in the regularity of movement and in the intensity of transnational connections. The mere availability of technological innovations does not indicate whether they are in fact used and, if they are, to what extent and how often. As Peter Kivisto points out, 'communication technologies do not determine how they are used; rather, the uses of technology are ultimately socially defined. Thus, it is important to explore not simply access to communication technologies, but also the ways different groups employ them' (Kivisto 2003: 15–16; see also Kivisto and Faist 2010: 156). For example, the social class of migrants and non-migrants is shaping the use of technology. Poor migrants might not be able to afford access to technologies equal to that of their middle- and upper-class counterparts. According to Alejandro Portes, 'immigrant communities with greater average economic resources and human capital (education and professional skills) should register higher levels of transnationalism because of their superior access to the infrastructure that makes these activities possible' (Portes et al. 1999: 224). Thus, in addition to transformations in transportation and communication technologies, the extent to which migrants and non-migrants have access to new technologies and the ways in which they are employed must also be considered. Furthermore, as Thomas Faist points out, 'improved methods of communication and travel set the necessary but not sufficient stage for the development of modern transnational ties' (Faist 2000a: 212). Accordingly, technology can be considered as the intervening variable, while the determining ones are the economic, political and cultural dynamics under which transnational practices in contemporary migration processes form and are maintained. The conditions shaping transnationalization include the globalization of capitalism (Glick Schiller et al. 1992b: 8–9) as well as changing circumstances within the countries of immigration and emigration, such as multicultural policies or the acceptance of dual citizenship (ibid.: 213–14; Foner 2001: 44–8; Smith 2003). The crucial role of ideology has been insufficiently recognized in this context. For example, in the age of nationalism in the early twentieth century there was not as much tolerance of citizens' transnational practices, either in the United States or in Europe, as there is today. Nationalism was connected to more rigid forms of assimilation, such as 'Americanization'. A very similar development can be noted with respect to the tolerance of dual nationality, unthinkable around the turn of the twentieth century but more accepted a hundred years later (see also chapter 6).

The concept of transnational social spaces

As the historical perspective outlined above points out, transnationality is not a new phenomenon in migration processes. However, alongside the technological transformations and economic, political and cultural dynamics, a changed scientific perspective in migration research contributed to the increased visibility of the transnational phenomenon from the early 1990s on. As Robert Smith states, 'if transnational life existed in the past but was not seen as such, then the transnational lens does new analytical work by providing a way of seeing what was there that could not be seen before because of a lack of lens to focus on it' (Smith 2003: 725). Thus, the 'transnational turn' does not refer primarily to new empirical evidence of transnationalization but rather constitutes a paradigmatic shift in migration research. A transnational lens faces methodological challenges and carries implications for the study of international migration. It is not only new terms that are being developed but also methodological tools and theoretical concepts to capture transnational social ties, processes and formations. Empirical case studies of transnationalization have yielded many observations concerning manifold cross-border practices. The theoretical strength of transnational perspectives lies in their challenge to traditional concepts in migration research, such as the classical understanding of assimilation (see chapter 5) and their critique of methodological nationalism and groupism (see chapter 7). Overall, transnational approaches have introduced an alternative analytical stance in migration studies. While there may not yet be a coherent theory of transnationalization, the concept of 'transnational social spaces' (Faist 2000a) in particular offers a heuristic tool for studying relations and practices of migrants and non-migrants across the borders of two or more nation-states.

Defining transnational social spaces

While transnational practices, as presented in chapter 2, may range along a continuum from low to high, transnational social spaces describe more concatenated cross-border ties and practices.

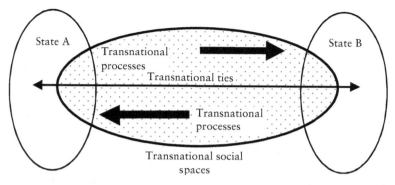

Figure 3.1   Transnational social spaces

Note: For reasons of presentation, transnational ties and practices are restricted in the figure to two states. Of course, transnational social spaces can extend across the borders of several states.

'By transnational spaces we mean relatively stable, lasting and dense sets of ties reaching beyond and across the borders of sovereign states. Transnational social spaces consist of combinations of ties and their contents, positions in networks and organizations, and networks of organizations that can be found in at least two geographically and internationally distinct places' (Faist 2000a: 197; see figure 3.1).

Most of these formations are located in between familial and personal practices and the functional systems of differentiated spheres, such as the familial, socio-cultural, economic and political. The smallest analytical units in a social space are social ties (Faist 2004a: 4). Social ties represent a sustaining and continuing series of pluri-local practices between at least two individuals. They can be manifested in social interaction among participants – for example, through migrants' visits to family members in the country of origin or in telephone calls to work colleagues abroad. But, going beyond social interactions and unique practices, social ties do not necessarily cease when there is a lack of co-presence but may reach beyond face-to-face relations between individuals – for example, through remittances of hometown associations supporting community projects in the country of emigration. Social ties often contain symbolic elements, such as common meanings, memories, future expectations and collective representation. When social ties of migrants and relatively immobile persons concatenate continuously and consistently, we speak of transnational social spaces. Even though a certain degree of stability and durability of social ties is necessary for their emergence, transnational social spaces are not static but are dynamic social processes (Faist 2000a: 199–200). Since they cut across the borders of at least two nation-states, transnational social spaces are distinct from clearly demarcated state territories (Faist 2004a: 4). Moreover, space is different from place in that it encompasses or spans various territorial locations and involves two or more places. Nor does the term 'social space' pertain only to physical features; it also has a social meaning that extends beyond simple territoriality. It refers to larger opportunity structures – the social life and the subjective images, values and meanings that the specific and limited place represents to migrants (Faist 2000a: 45–6). By embracing two or more nation-states, international migrants and non-migrants living in transnational social spaces form networks, groups and 'communities without propinquity' (Webber 1963). The reality of transnational social spaces indicates, first, that migration and remigration may not signify definite, irrevocable and irreversible decisions. Transnational lives themselves may become a strategy of survival and betterment. Second, even those migrants who have settled for a considerable time outside their country of origin may frequently entertain strong transnational social ties and practices (Faist 2000a: 200).

As shown above, processes of migration and transnationalization are shaped by transformations in technology as well as by economic, political and cultural dynamics in the countries of immigration and emigration. Against this background, transnational social spaces develop in two stages (Faist 2000a: 201). In a first phase they are a by-product of international migration and seem to be limited basically to the first generation of migrants. Researchers have long recognized that migration is not simply a transfer from one place to another with few social and material links between the two. Rather, migration usually generates continuous exchanges between geographically distant communities, and migrants do not automatically sever their social ties to the countries of emigration. In a second phase of development, transnational social spaces appear to go beyond the strictly migratory chains of the first generation of migrants and develop a life of their own. This should be seen in the context of generational succession. The phenomenon of transnationalization may not be limited to the first generation of migrants. Even the succeeding generations, as documented by the case studies of Emre, Kamber and Adnan in chapter 2, can sustain transnational ties and develop their own new forms of border-crossing links (see also chapter 5). To take only one example from the economic sphere of life, in Germany there has been a shift from the remittances of the first-generation migrants to ethnic businesses and further to direct investment in Turkey by second-generation Turkish entrepreneurs. While these transnational enterprises relocate their production to Turkey, the administration and distribution of products takes place in Germany.

Types of transnational social spaces

Persons engaged in transnational practices do not necessarily have sustained social ties to one another. There are also unique get-togethers between strangers or ad hoc encounters without formal membership or a sense of belonging. For example, entrepreneurs previously unknown to one another may meet in the marketplace for a one-time exchange of goods, capital and services. Another example would be holiday-makers who interact at a tourist resort without having further contact with each other. Over time, however, transnational social ties and practices can concatenate in transnational social spaces. Using the examples already mentioned, entrepreneurs may develop their business relationship or the vacation acquaintances may exchange letters after spending their holiday together. Taking the density of social ties as a point of departure, in total three ideal types of transnational social spaces characterized by typical forms of social resources can be distinguished (Faist 2000a: 202–10): reciprocity in transnational kinship groups, exchange in transnational circuits and solidarity in transnational communities (see table 3.1).

Table 3.1   Types of transnational social spaces

	Primary resources in ties	*Main characteristic*	*Typical examples*
Transnational kinship groups	*Reciprocity:* what one party receives from the other requires something in return	Upholding the *social norm* of equivalence; control over members of small groups	*Remittances* of household or family members from country of immigration to country of emigration – e.g., contract workers
Transnational circuits	*Exchange:* mutual obligations and expectations of the actors; outcome of instrumental activity – e.g., the tit-for-tat principle	Exploitation of *insider advantages*: language; strong and weak social ties in peer networks	*Trading networks*, e.g., Chinese, Lebanese, and Indian business people
Transnational communities	*Solidarity:* shared ideas, beliefs, values and symbols expressed in some sort of collective identity	Mobilization of *collective representations* within (abstract) symbolic ties – e.g., religion, nationality, ethnicity	*Diasporas:* e.g., Jews, Armenians, Palestinians, Kurds

Transnational kinship groups
Highly formalized cross-border ties within small groups such as households and families, or even wider kinship systems, are typical of many migrants, especially in the first generation. Core or extended families may live apart because one or more members work abroad as contract workers (for instance, the former guest workers in Germany) or as expatriates within multinational

companies. Transnational kinship groups have a strong sense of belonging to a common home. A classic example is transnational families who conceive of themselves as both an economic and a social unit. Transnational kinship groups make use of resources inherent in social ties like reciprocity. Reciprocity means that what one party receives from the other requires some return. The involvement of the participants is thus characterized by clearly identifiable rights and obligations. Reciprocity is expressed, for example, in financial remittances from migrants to their families in the countries of emigration for the purpose of improving their living conditions. Other typical transnational practices in kinship groups include familial practices such as care of children and the elderly. This type of transnational social space may be retained only until core families are reunited in one country or if family members abroad die. But transnational kinship groups can also be more enduring, as for example in the case of extended family ties.

Transnational circuits

Transnational circuits are sets of social ties between persons and organizations in which the exchange of resources takes place for the purpose of achieving a common goal. This includes, for example, the exchange of information or services. Linkage patterns may concatenate into advocacy networks, business networks or science networks. There is a long tradition of transnational circuits in the realm of human rights, and they are making steady progress in ecology; now they are also emerging among migrants who have moved from one country to another. Often, there is a common discourse around a specific focus such as human rights or professional issues, and such networks and organizations are sometimes even seen as the nucleus of a 'global civil society' (Keane 2003; see also chapter 8). Typical transnational practices undertaken by migrants aimed at specific issues include frequent exchanges of folkloristic dance groups or artists. As to business networks, migrants abroad constitute an important source of financial transfer and investment, both as entrepreneurs in the country of immigration and in cooperation with their countries of origin. The governments of emigration states have increasingly initiated programmes to attract emigrants' investments. Among the most dense set of transnational networks – a set of interlinked local, national and regional networks – in the world are those of the overseas Chinese and Indians abroad, which promote trade by providing market information and matching and referral services by using their co-ethnic ties. Such social ties alleviate the problems associated with contract enforcement and provide information about trading opportunities.

Transnational communities

Communities constitute highly formalized types of transnational social spaces with an inherent potential for a relatively long life span. Close social ties with symbolic elements are characteristic of transnational communities. Solidarity exists in larger 'we-groups' where members cannot cultivate all relationships personally and directly. Thus, solidarity is expressed in some sort of collective identity. Transnational communities comprise dense and continuous sets of social ties, characterized by a high degree of intimacy, emotional depth, moral obligation and social cohesion. They can evolve at different levels of aggregation. The simplest type consists of village communities in cross-border migration systems, whose relations are marked by solidarity extended over long periods of time. Typical transnational practices are investments in private or public projects for the benefits of the community in question undertaken by members who are abroad or have returned home. The quintessential form of transnational communities consists of larger cross-border religious groups and churches. The major world religions – Judaism, Christianity, Islam, Hinduism and Buddhism – existed long before modern states came into existence. Furthermore, diasporas also belong to the category of transnational communities (e.g., Brubaker 2005). In classical renditions, these are groups that experienced the territorial dispersion of their members some time in the past, either as a result of a traumatic experience or in pursuit of long-distance trade. Jews, Palestinians, Armenians and Greeks can be cited as examples here. Generally, members of diasporas have a common memory of their lost homeland or a vision of one to be created, while at the same time the country of immigration often refuses the respective minority full acknowledgement of its cultural distinctiveness (Gold 2002; see also chapters 6 and 8).

Dynamics of transnational social spaces

As already mentioned, transnational social spaces are not to be seen as static units but as socially constituted. It is thus of prime importance to let go of fixed notions of social formations and their boundaries (see also chapter 7 for a critique on methodological nationalism and groupism). Rather, the focus is on how the boundaries in transnational social spaces themselves come into existence and change. 'By transnational, we propose an optic or gaze that begins with a world without borders, empirically examines the boundaries and borders that emerge at particular historical moments, and explores their relationship to unbounded arenas and processes' (Khagram and Levitt 2008: 5). Thus, beginning with a dynamic approach to transnational social spaces offers the chance to look at changing boundaries – in relation to existing ones (for example, nation-states) and to new ones (emergent properties of transnational and global systems) – and to explore how old spaces are transformed and new spaces emerge. To understand how boundaries in transnational social spaces change and are redrawn, reinforced or transformed, the social mechanisms at work in the making and unmaking of boundaries need to be analysed (see Faist 2009: 80–6). Thomas Faist (ibid.: 77) identifies four ways in which boundaries are being redrawn (inspired by the typology in Zolberg and Woon 1999).

1 Existing boundaries become porous, as in the case of dual citizenship – when more and more nation-states tolerate overlapping membership of nations (see chapter 6).
2 Boundaries may shift, as when lines between 'us' and 'them' no longer run along national lines but along religious ones. This has happened in many states in Western Europe over the past three decades. Public debates there refer to conflicts not

between nationalities but between Muslims and 'us' as relevant trench lines.

3   Boundaries can be maintained or even reinforced, as in the extension of border control in the European Union to the patrolling of exterior borders, the emergence of buffer zones with adjacent countries, and an increase in controls internal to nation-states (e.g., Zaiotti 2011).

4   New boundaries emerge, as evidenced by the portrayal of and public policies towards transnational practices.

While transnational practices of highly skilled and prosperous migrants are celebrated by immigration states and increasingly also emigration states as a significant contribution to the competitiveness of national economies, the transnational ties of other categories, such as so-called low-skilled migrants, are often seen as contributing to segregation and self-exclusion. Or, to give another example, transnational social ties may represent a security risk, as in the case of terrorist networks, or a boon to development, as in the case of international migrants with resource-rich social ties. The exact mechanisms of boundary genesis and changes need to be researched in order to gauge how new societal formations emerge across borders but also in what ways well-entrenched institutions such as nation-states and international organizations change and adapt. To sum up, the concept of transnational social spaces requires a dynamic approach which considers the question of the emergence of such spaces on the basis of empirical evidence.

The durability of transnationalization

So far, research has not provided a definitive answer to the question of whether transnationalization and transnational social spaces are enduring or just temporary phenomena and whether they will last for more than one or two generations (Faist 2000a: 239). As a result of migration from one nation-state to another, many migrants are spatially separated from their family members, relatives and friends who remain in the country of origin. In some cases migrants spend their entire life in another country. In other cases the separation lasts only a limited period of time until the border is crossed again in one direction or the other, leading to family reunification in the country of immigration or to return migration. While some assimilation theorists assume that cross-border social ties and practices would not endure through the medium- or long-term, either because of the integration process in the country of immigration or through return migration (see also chapter 5), transnational approaches point out that – even if this is not the case for all migrants – migration processes lead to the formation of transnational social spaces. From this perspective, transnational relations and practices do not necessarily decrease with the duration of stay in the new country. As Thomas Faist (2000a: 200) points out, 'even those migrants and refugees who have settled for a considerable time outside the country of origin frequently entertain strong transnational links.' Other transnational studies actually go a step further in arguing against decreasing contacts by stating that 'people with longer time in the United States are more likely to participate in transnational activities' (Itzigsohn and Saucedo 2002: 784; see also Portes et al. 2002: 289). As with long periods of residence, return migration does not necessarily lead to a decrease in transnational involvement. For example, drawing on the case of Germany and Turkey, it is shown that migrants can continue transnational practices by using migration experiences as a resource for establishing transnational businesses when they returned to their country of origin (Dişbudak 2004).

This raises not only the question of how durable the phenomenon of transnationalization in general is but also of how durable different degrees of transnationality are and how they become transformed, both during the life course and over generations. So far, however, 'few longitudinal studies explore how transnational practices change over time or the extent to which they remain salient beyond the first generation' (Levitt 2001b: 196). It has been shown that transnational practices can be carried on continuously, but they can also decrease or increase over the lifetime of individuals. In some cases migrants basically continue to engage in a range of practices related to their home country after moving to and becoming integrated into their new country. The maintenance of ties to family and friends still residing in the country of emigration can remain fairly stable over time, or they can 'ebb and flow at different stages of individuals' life cycles' (Levitt 2001a: 20; see also Levitt and Glick Schiller 2004: 1012–13), which is more likely. Thus, the intensity of transnational practices varies not only among migrants themselves and between different spheres of social life, as shown in chapter 2, but also throughout individual life spans. For example, increasing transnational practices are observable for migrants who circulate between two countries after retirement, while the death of a relative abroad can lead to decreasing transnationality. To gain further insight into life-course effects, more research is necessary on 'how the relationships between those migrating abroad and those who stayed in the country of origin have developed, altered, declined, or strengthened' (Faist 2000a: 46). Moreover, the particular opportunities and restrictions which lead to periodical involvement in transnational practices need to be determined. For example, changes in the migrant's financial situation during different stages of the life cycle can create decreasing but also increasing transnationality. Overall, this glimpse into transnational practices from a biographical perspective already illustrates that transnationality is not static but variable over the course of time (for the dynamic of transnationality, see also Fauser and Reisenauer 2012).

The process character of transnationality is obvious not only for the life course but also with regard to generations (on the issue of second-generation transnationality, see especially chapter 5). Transnational approaches raise the question as to whether transnationality is a phenomenon characteristic only of immigrants or whether it also exists beyond this first generation of migrants. To clarify the endurance of transnationality over generations, transnational studies increasingly look at both the immigrant generation and the subsequent generations. Thus a general distinction is made between children of migrants who were born in the country of emigration but who grew up and were socialized in the country of immigration – the so-called in-between or 1.5 generation – and those who were born in the new country and have no experience of migration – the so-called second generation. Whether or not transnationality has significance for these 1.5 and second generations is a controversial question for those employing transnational perspectives. Critics claim that there is no evidence at present that transnationality is transmitted intergenerationally: 'By and large, regular involvement in transnational activities appears to be a one-generation phenomenon, at least in the United States. However, this involvement can have resilient effects on the second generation both through its influence on the socio-economic integration of parents and through the latter's persistent efforts to create "bridges" between their children and the culture and communities left behind' (Portes 2001: 190). While the study by Alejandro Portes suggests that children of immigrants are affected only indirectly by the transnational practices of their parents, other studies come to the conclusion there is involvement in transnational life among the 1.5 and second generations (e.g., Levitt and Waters 2002). Even if the majority is rooted in the country of their parents and their participation is less obvious compared with that of their parents, there is an important proportion of the 1.5 and second generations contributing to transnationalization (Levitt 2002). Children of immigrant families are initially left behind in the care of grandparents or other relatives while their parents work and live abroad and are brought to the country of immigration when they are older; or they are born in the country to which their parents have immigrated but are sent 'home' to be raised there. These cases illustrate that children of migrants grow up within transnational social spaces. They may circulate back and forth and live significant periods of their life in two countries. They might return with their families for vacations or important events, such as baptisms or marriages, and they may maintain relations with grandparents or other relatives left behind. Some of those children continue their transnational involvement into adult life – for example, by marrying someone who lives in the country of emigration (Strassburger 2004; Beck-Gernsheim 2006; Schmidt 2011). Another phenomenon that is attracting the attention of scholars is so-called second-generation return (King and Christou 2010b). While there is some research into the involvement of 1.5

and second generations in transnational social spaces, we need to learn more about the extent to which subsequent generations maintain transnational relationships and how they differ from first-generation forms of transnational life. To explore the issue of the transformation of transnationality in the course of time, concerning both individual biographies and across generations, transnational approaches have to go beyond studies at a single point in time by carrying out longitudinal research (Portes et al. 2002: 294).[5]

4

Transnationalization and Development

Development is a prominent field in which the changes brought about by transnationalization can be observed. In this respect, the new visibility of migrants' transnationality and the emergence of transnational social spaces have renewed interest in the nexus between migration and development in both fields of study, as well as on the part of policy stakeholders, heads of state and international agencies such as the United Nations and the World Bank. Although the relationship between migration and development has been debated for many decades, today the transnational ties and practices of migrants play a much more crucial role in that debate. For instance, monetary remittances receive great attention, as they support the family a migrant has left behind and benefit people's well-being and social security. Remittances are also invested in business ventures and small-scale transnational companies and transferred as collective contributions for the local development of home villages. The circulation of information is another important issue, and the emergence of cross-border knowledge networks of migrants and diasporic groups has contributed to the circulation of skills and expertise and thus to 'brain gain' in both developed and developing countries. This has sometimes reversed the negative effect of 'brain drain' caused by highly educated physicians, engineers and academics leaving developing countries for the developed world. In addition, the exchange of ideas, norms and behaviour, collectively termed social remittances (Levitt 1998), is increasingly acknowledged in more and more research and in policy papers and documents such as the *Human Development Report* (UNDP 2009). Social remittances are exchanged through communication, visits or the return of migrants to their home villages, where they may become an element of social and cultural and even political change. Through these exchanges, norms and standards concerning gender hierarchies or the environment may change, and experiences abroad have led migrants to challenge clientelist practices previously considered common to daily life in their home community (see chapter 2). This complex of ties, activities and spaces spanning state borders thus calls for a transnational perspective in order to grasp the economic and social transformations generally associated today with development around the world (Faist and Fauser 2011).

Although the debate on the migration–development nexus is not new, transnationalization is a fresh aspect in this field, and this contributed to a reconsideration of some earlier standpoints held by scholars and politicians (Faist 2008). While there was initially a positive perspective on return and investment, in the 1970s and 1980s more critical voices were raised as to the negative effects for the countries of emigration, particularly through brain drain. Today, once again, in academia and the political realm, the positive relationship of the migration–development nexus is more dominant. Migrants' transnational ties and transfers are seen as carrying enormous potential to reduce poverty, overcome underdevelopment and eventually stop migration of ever more people.

Hence, this chapter explains the role of transnationalization for development. The next section describes the three major phases of change in the migration–development nexus and examines the way in which transnational ties, practices and spaces have become a key issue in this relationship, both in academia and among policy stakeholders. The chapter then addresses the role of transnationalization for a broader set of development issues among the different types of transnational social spaces (transnational kinship, circuits and communities). Here, we look first at the flow of financial remittances and the implications of such flows on the level of family and kinship groups. Second, the economic impact of remittances through transnational circuits and business networks is considered. Third, the important issue of hometown associations as part of transnational communities and their role in local development is discussed. Fourth, we describe the circulation of knowledge, which has become a major issue for the development of information- and knowledge-based societies. Finally, the chapter addresses the role of social remittances for socio-cultural and political change. It must be stressed that the notion of development as employed here carries a multiplicity of meanings along its socio-economic, political and human dimensions. These range from economic growth and political (democratic) change, equality and human rights to the livelihoods of individuals and families. Therefore, the chapter takes up the different meanings of development rather than employing one specific conceptualization. This is also to say that, in the current debate, development is located in countries of emigration, whereas the relationship between migrants and their new countries is generally discussed more from a perspective of their integration (see chapter 5) and less in terms of their contributions to development there. A more comprehensive analysis would require looking at the development contributions in countries of immigration as well.

Three phases of the debate

Development as a discourse and policy field was established in the aftermath of the Second World War, and since then the notion of development has been associated with different meanings from the various theoretical vantage points in the field. It has meant, variously, great transformation, modernization and economic growth; asymmetric power relationships and dependency in the world system; and livelihoods of people measured by human development indicators; and it is referred to as democratic government and good governance. In the same vein, the relationship between migration and development has been addressed from different perspectives, beneficial as well as negative. Three phases can be distinguished in this regard.

In the first phase, in the 1950s and 1960s, economic theories envisaged that migrants would fill labour shortages in the countries of immigration and at the same time, through financial remittances, savings and the eventual return of migrants, contribute to development in the countries of emigration. Schemes for the temporary recruitment of migrant workers followed on this thinking: all the governments involved shared a perspective that migrants should move to work temporarily in the booming industries of the postwar economies of the US (through the Bracero Program from 1942 to 1964) and Europe (through guest-worker schemes, mainly in the 1960s and early 1970s), to earn sufficient money to sustain their families, who normally remained back home, and, by the time they returned, to have saved enough to improve their living standards and increase job opportunities through their new skills and investments.

In the second phase, some critical voices became more prominent, and migration often came to be seen as negatively affecting societies and economies in the countries of origin. In the 1970s and 1980s, structural dependency between industrialized Western countries and peripheral world regions constituted a major explanation for underdevelopment (Wallerstein 1974; Frank 1978). Migration was yet another factor serving to deplete resources from the periphery to the benefit of the centre of the capitalist world system, especially when it involved well-educated people. Although the original term 'brain drain' is now often replaced by 'brain gain' and 'knowledge circulation', this issue still is a matter of concern for many governments of developing countries, as will be discussed below in the section on transnational circulation of knowledge. Out-migration is also often problematic for rural areas when those who leave are the young and the able-bodied (Lipton 1980; De Haas 2008). In this phase, remittances came to be seen more negatively as well, because they were frequently found to contribute little to development, being spent on 'conspicuous consumption' in the form of prestigious houses and luxurious festivities. Moreover, some authors observed that households had become dependent on remittances, which contributed to recurrent migration in order to maintain that source of income – a phenomenon which has been called the 'migrant syndrome' (Reichert 1981; Durand et al. 1996: 437). Ironically, in the second phase this critical evaluation dovetailed with the restrictions on immigration imposed in Western countries in the 1970s in the face of the oil crises and the onset of economic recession (Faist 2011).

In the third phase, starting in the mid-1990s, the assessment changed dramatically, and the focus, rather than being on return, is now on cross-border exchanges. Here new actors, called 'transnational communities' and 'diasporas', make their entrance on the stage (Goldring 2004). Migrants have come to be seen as agents of development, an idea which is now frequently expressed by the French term *co-développement* (co-development) (Naïr 1997). In this phase, migrants became part of many policy initiatives in the realm of development aid and cooperation. Again policy proposals and academic debate conflate with an optimistic view of their development contributions (Faist 2011). The circulation of people, through temporary and circular migration, the cross-border transfer of remittances and the flows of knowledge and ideas attract great attention in academia and among policy stakeholders.

Empirical studies have revealed mixed outcomes, however, when it comes to the effects of migration on the development of different regions. Existing research identifies a broad range of contextual factors influencing outcomes which makes broader generalizations thus far particularly difficult, as will become clear throughout this chapter. What is important (and new in this phase) is the existence of continued cross-border movement and the transnational practices of migrants. Therefore the current processes at the nexus of migration and development need to be addressed from a transnational perspective as well.

Remittances and their role for family and kin

Cross-border financial transfers in the form of remittances stand at the centre of the current debate on migration–development linkages and of policy efforts at the local, national and global scales

Table 4.1   The top ten remittances-receiving countries

By amount (US$ billion), 2010		By percentage of GDP, 2009	
1 India	55.0	1 Tajikistan	35
2 China	51.0	2 Tonga	28
3 Mexico	22.6	3 Lesotho	25
4 Philippines	21.3	4 Moldova	23
5 France	15.9	5 Nepal	23
6 Germany	11.6	6 Lebanon	22
7 Bangladesh	11.1	7 Samoa	22
8 Belgium	10.4	8 Honduras	19
9 Spain	10.2	9 Guyana	17
10 Nigeria	10.0	10 El Salvador	16

Source: World Bank (2011: 13–14).

(see chapter 1). The amount of money sent home by migrants has been reaching unprecedented levels over the past two decades. Remittances transferred to developing countries through official channels rose from US$40 billion in 1990 to $167 billion in 2005, and to $338 billion in the year 2008 (IOM 2005; World Bank 2009). Although official development assistance from OECD countries has also been growing and reached its highest amount ever recorded in 2008, at $119.8 billion (OECD 2009), officially recorded remittance flows were still three times higher. What is not included in those figures is money sent through other channels, the so-called informal monetary transfer systems which exist on a global scale among some migrant communities, such as the *hawala* among South Asians or the Chinese *fei ch'ien*. Through these systems migrants send money via agents who, in turn, instruct counterparts in the regions where the recipients live (Kapur 2004). Money is also transferred by individual couriers or by the migrants themselves simply carrying their earned dollars and euros with them on visits back home.

The four countries receiving the highest sums of remittances in the year 2010 were India, China, Mexico and the Philippines, but the top ten list also includes various Western European countries (see table 4.1). In twenty-two countries of the world the share of remittances is 10 per cent or more of gross domestic product (GDP); in first-ranked Tajikistan, remittances make up 35 per cent of GDP. Those receiving such remittances are (with the exception of Serbia and Bosnia-Herzegovina) developing and non-Western countries, where the economic importance of such financial transfers is highest (World Bank 2011). In many countries, it is not only the total amount and average share of remittances that is high; the amounts of money migrants sent back home to their families and kin are often of a relatively broad scope and reach many households. Studies estimate that, in Mexico, more than 1 million households – that is, over 5 per cent of the total number of households – receive remittances (Goldring 2004: 802). In smaller countries, and especially in the Caribbean and Pacific islands with high numbers of emigrants, the share of households affected by financial transfers is much greater. For instance, in Cape Verde, around two-thirds of all families receive money from their relatives abroad (Kapur 2004).

The impact of remittances is still contested. The literature agrees that the majority of those monetary transfers in fact serve as income. They are spent on current consumption for household maintenance – that is, food and clothing, health care, home construction and remodelling, and consumer goods (Durand et al. 1996; Goldring 2004; Kapur 2004). Only a small proportion is in fact put directly into local and national economies constituting productive investment with long-term consequences. Therefore, the impact and economic potential of migration and the money sent back home by migrants have been judged to be minor.

At the level of the family, the new economics of labour migration (NELM) approach specifically highlights the crucial role of remittances which serve as income, motivating migration in the first place as a strategy of income diversification and poverty alleviation. Here, migration is considered a livelihood strategy (Nyberg-Sørensen et al. 2002). In the NELM approach (Stark and Lucas 1988),[6] remittances form part of a contractual arrangement mobilizing cooperation within the family in order to minimize risks and provide security for its members. Taking into account two-way flows, the approach points out that the migrant receives financial support to establish and overcome difficult circumstances such as unemployment (ibid.: 467). Her or his principal role, however, is to improve the socio-economic situation of the family. A household survey in the Mexican state of Zacatecas reveals that, in rural areas, where family income was below average, those families who had ties to one or more migrants and who received remittances had a higher income both overall and relative to that of families in urban areas (Jones 1998).

In this view, remittances are often considered as a way through which migrants from poor households and underdeveloped world regions counteract their marginalized status and 'equalize income among nations in the current global economy' (Jones 1998: 8). But the impact can sometimes also be negative, as it may lead to dependency on remittances – hence the 'migrant syndrome' (see above; Reichert 1981). In addition, greater inequality can result from the fact that not all families in a village will have a migrant among their kin, and so will not receive money from abroad. Thus, those who do receive financial support may be able to improve their socio-economic situation, while for those who do not the gap widens. Because of the selectivity of migration, remittances are also selective (Jones 1998); social inequalities may continue and even deepen because it is generally the better-off families who send migrants abroad, and it is these families therefore that are more likely than poor households to receive remittances.

The role of financial transfers is especially prominent in times of severe crisis affecting migrants' families back home, when remittances were found to increase (Kapur 2004) and thus reduce the vulnerability of poor households. Yet, when the crisis is of global scope, affecting both countries of emigration and immigration, and especially the sectors in which migrants work, remittances tend to decrease, as was observed during the latest financial and economic crisis (Fix et al. 2009). The contribution of remittances to poverty alleviation is therefore dependent on complex contextual factors. Moreover, such a perspective requires a notion of development defined not only by economic growth but also by socio-economic and human development and a focus on the livelihoods of people.

Transnational investment and business

The overall impact of remittances on national and local economic development has remained unclear, but economic investment through remittances could be greater than has thus far been acknowledged. On the one hand, the money spent on food, clothing or consumer goods has indirect effects on local and national economies, in that it creates a demand for certain products, services and professions. On the other hand, only a fraction of all remittances is used for investment in economic enterprises. Yet, a number of government initiatives in recent years aim to support productive investment in the local and national economies of migrants, and the assumption is that these are likely to contribute to both growth and effectiveness.

Exploring the economically productive use of remittances in Mexico, Durand, Parrado and Massey (1996) have pointed to the demand created by local expenditure on consumption. Their study found that both the food and the clothing bought with remittances were produced mainly in Mexico. The material required for the newly built houses of migrants' families were primarily home-produced, too. In addition, the availability of 'migradollars' in Mexican villages and towns generated new demands for physicians, pharmacists, teachers and architects. Even the celebration of patron saints' festivities in the villages supported and financed through migrants' transnationality involved large quantities of food, drink, music and fireworks, thus requiring production and services from the local market. Furthermore, the availability of additional income for households has allowed poorer rural families to invest capital in new technology, so that agricultural production has become more efficient. Using pumps and farm machinery, rural Mexican farmers started to harvest twice a year and were able to produce food beyond subsistence needs which they could sell on the local market, thus generating new income. Through these spending patterns, remittances create multiplier effects above the level of the amount of the money transferred. This study estimated the effects of expenditure on consumption, together with direct investment, at a rate 3.25 times the value of 'migradollars' transferred to Mexico.

In addition, a certain share of remittances is invested in business, which is increasingly supported by national and local authorities from many different places across the world. 'Invest in Mexico' is one of these programmes through which governments engage with migrants' transnationality. It is operated by the Mexican National Development Bank and financed through a fund from the Inter-American Development Bank (Goldring 2004). In a similar vein, public officials and representatives from local chambers of commerce in Turkey encourage business ventures from Turkish migrants abroad as an important source of foreign investment (Çağlar 2006). Still rarely heeded – and most difficult to enumerate – are the many more private business arrangements maintained transnationally by migrants with family members and friends in the country of origin, and not always in the home village. These are frequently not channelled through official banking and financial institutions. Arrangements observed among Ghanaian migrants in Amsterdam include a case where a car bought in Europe was shipped to Ghana, where it serves as a taxi, providing a stable income for both the driver and the family of the migrant who sent the car back home; in another case, 100 euros sent from a migrant friend were enough for a young woman from Accra to become a partner in a small-scale business. In other instances, financial support for a business serves merely to compensate for an unprofitable shop but ensures other reciprocal commitments within the family (Smith 2011). Other examples are mobile and non-mobile migrants engaged in transnational small-scale businesses such as the export of electronic items from Germany to Ghana or the establishment and management from abroad of small service companies (Bühlmeier et al. 2011).

Hometown associations and their contributions to community development

In addition to providing family income and business investments, remittances circulate at the collective or community level (Goldring 2004). Village and hometown associations (HTAs) constitute a growing sector of non-state actors that has recently been shown to have significance for development (Faist 2008). These associations are tangible signs of the existence of transnational communities tying migrants and non-migrants together. The functions these associations fulfil range from social exchange and political influence to low-scale and local development goals in home villages (Orozco and Lapointe 2004: 31). The occurrence of Mexican HTAs in the US has attracted the most attention so far, not least because of their sheer number – amounting to at least 2,000. In Los Angeles alone, a total of 170 HTAs from eighteen Mexican states were already officially registered with the Mexican consulate more than ten years ago (Zabin and Escala 2002). Similarly, the Salvadoran government estimates that in the mid-2000s there were 250 HTAs outside the country, whereas ten years previously there had probably been no more than twenty-eight (Waldinger et al. 2008). Many migrant communities in other world regions have developed similar forms of organization. And, although most research to date has been undertaken on associations located in the US, collective cross-border activities also exist among immigrant communities in France, the UK, Germany, Spain and Italy and engage migrants from Turkey, Morocco, Latin America, sub-Saharan Africa and the Indian subcontinent (Grillo and Riccio 2004; Lacroix 2005; Mercer et al. 2009; Fauser 2011).

Hometown associations are a grassroots and philanthropic phenomenon, part of emerging transnational social movements and an expression of transnationalizing civil society (see chapter 8; Sassen 2002; Orozco and Lapointe 2004). They build on ties and networks that connect migrants abroad to their place of origin, beyond the circle of family and kin. These associations collect money and raise funds in order to develop projects aimed at bettering the situation in their hometowns. Although such collective efforts have always existed, they are currently intensifying and becoming more institutionalized, with the number of associations still on the rise. Their financial contributions are generally charitable donations and often support investment in local infrastructure. The projects supported by HTAs generally fall into one of the following domains (Goldring 2004):

- basic infrastructure and communication projects, such as roads, bridges and potable water, telephone and (these days) internet cafés, which allow villagers to stay in touch with migrants abroad
- public service infrastructure and capitalization related to education, health or social security – that is, schools, computers, ambulances, food baskets and support for children's school lunch programmes
- recreation and other more status-related projects, such as sports fields, rodeo rings and other community projects such as halls, public spaces, benches, and the preservation of cultural heritage and churches.

Depending on the region and type of association, some projects are also focused on agriculture and cultivation or local production of other goods. Such investments are often meant to benefit marginalized groups of villagers (unemployed, handicapped or poor women) rather than being profit-oriented. Emigration states have manifested an increasing interest in maintaining knowledge about these associations and in staying in contact with them. Their governments call upon migrants' loyalties, and representatives at both the national and the local level encourage their collective investment. Various institutions in countries of immigration and development aid agencies have followed suit and also offer support and assistance to migrants' efforts (see also chapters 2 and 6).

HTAs can be considered the institutionalized expression of transnational communities spanning various locations across state borders (Goldring 2004). This should not, however, lead to their being considered in idealized images. On the one hand, scholars have pointed out that only a limited number of migrants are involved in these organizations. On the other hand, the cooperation between those abroad and those who stay behind tends to be asymmetric, which casts doubt on the idea that HTAs were an expression of a homogeneous transnational community. With respect to the first concern, there exists little systematic evidence on the proportion of migrants involved in HTAs. Available data suggest that the circle of active participants in collective transnational organizations comprises only a minority of all migrants. Others, however, join in on occasion – through more irregular donations, for example (Guarnizo et al. 2003: table 3, 1227). Exploring the characteristics of the participants and especially the members of these organizations, numerous studies point out that men are predominant and few women are involved in their daily activities, although there exists little systematic research in this regard (Portes et al. 2007; Sieveking et al. 2008). Also it is usually first-generation immigrants, and less frequently the younger and second generations, who are active: where younger people born in the country of immigration are involved, they are guided by a different motivation and by different ideas on how to run such an organization. In a study by Sieveking and Fauser (2009) on Malian HTAs located in France, representatives of various organizations emphasized the distinction between the different generations with regard to the motivation and strategies for their engagement. Those in the first generation – people who had themselves migrated and were still close to the family and kin they had left behind – brought together their own money saved from their modest salaries for community projects in their villages. The second generation is seen as more professional in the planning of projects and the raising of money. Their organizations prepare feasibility studies and undertake more elaborate cost calculations before starting a project in order to achieve greater efficiency. The emerging third generation engaged in these organizations, in turn, is no longer considered African but rather European, with few personal ties to their grandparents' communities of origin. These activists do not contribute their own money towards projects but help to establish cooperative relations with other actors in France and support fund-raising activities. They are thus becoming partners in development cooperation rather than forming part of a transnational village community.

This leads to the second concern, which questions the community character of HTAs. Research has revealed considerable tensions within associations, especially between the members at home and those abroad. Often perspectives differ in regard to the goal of the contributions, the types of projects to support and how to spend the money, and the degree and form of participation and cooperation. Frequent disputes arise around the question of how intensively to collaborate with the authorities (Levitt 1997; Waldinger et al. 2008). Some studies also document that such internal conflicts and disagreements on the principles of collaboration have led to the splitting up of an organization. Over the course of time, especially, tensions become more pronounced when migrants and villagers develop different priorities. Peggy Levitt (1997, 2001a) found in her study on the development committee operating between Boston and Miraflores in the Dominican Republic that, with the progression of settlement, the concern of absentees was more with their vacations and retirement, and their interests shifted towards cultural programmes and other traditional and folkloristic aspects. Those who stayed in Miraflores, in turn, were more interested in local economic development which would generate jobs, in youth programmes and in better sport facilities. Here, as in many other cases, the relationship between migrants and non-migrants is characterized by a donor–beneficiary relationship rather than a collaboration of partners and equal members of one community.

Although the notion of community may sometimes be contested in these endeavours, HTAs nevertheless signal new transnational formations and generally reaffirm migrants' membership in their places of origin (Goldring 2004). This is expressed not only through their financial contributions. Associations and their leaders can also acquire considerable political leverage, especially in smaller villages, where their contributions are of great significance and often exceed public budgets. In many small rural Mexican communities, for instance, donations from HTAs were seven times the local budget assigned to public work (Orozco and Lapointe 2004: 39). Mayors, governors and other public officials and politicians from these villages go to visit 'their' local migrant communities abroad to discuss new projects and to campaign during elections. It is in this context that policy-makers have become more receptive to the claims of migrants, which in turn led to an expansion of their extraterritorial rights. Local participation, extraterritorial voting rights and dual citizenship have been extended across the world, thus further strengthening transnational communities and other formations as well as individual cross-border ties (see chapter 6).

The interest shown in collective remittances by governments from countries of emigration, as well as international donors and other institutions from countries of immigration, along with their support for the role of HTAs, can be seen as 'the consolidation of a development model which emphasizes the market and public–private partnerships as arrangements that enable market integration' (Goldring 2004: 809). Migrants' transnational networks now form part of a broader reorientation in development thinking that includes community, or civil society, along with states and markets (Faist 2008). Networks of other kinds have emerged among scientists and other highly skilled migrants where the circulation of knowledge is a primary goal, as shall be shown below.

Transnational circulation of knowledge

The flow of knowledge across state borders has become a key issue in the era of information- and knowledge-based societies. Accordingly, the emigration of highly qualified professionals and the brain drain from generally less developed countries has always attracted great concern among heads of state as well as development economists, and not only from a dependency-theory perspective on underdevelopment. Originally coined in the 1950s by the British Royal Society to describe the flow of scientists from Europe to North America, 'brain drain' today refers to the flow of highly skilled migrants from less to more developed countries (Lowell et al. 2004). This notion expresses a concern for the negative impacts of out-migration for countries of origin and especially the hampering of prospects for their economic development. The migration of qualified professionals, like many other migratory flows, was long considered a one-way process terminating with settlement for the migrants and human capital gains for the country of immigration. For the country of emigration it meant a loss of human capital and corresponding brain drain. Although it is sometimes suggested that financial remittances had the potential to outweigh the negative effects of brain drain, this assumption is not sustained by evidence (Jones 1998; Kapur 2004). The balance is even less positive when considering that remittances also flow both ways, and that developed countries receive a greater share of them – for instance, in the form of fees for higher education from students from developing countries (Khadria 2002). Today, more circular movements of people and the associated two-way flows of knowledge, skills and ideas are attracting increasing attention as they contribute to considerable economic innovations (Findlay 1995; Hunger 2003; Lowell et al. 2004). Brain gain resulting from the circulation of knowledge has emerged as an opportunity for developing countries.

According to a growing number of studies, two elements play a role in the positive contribution of highly skilled migration to development: return and 'diasporic' networks (Meyer et al. 1997; Meyer 2001; Hunger 2003). The return of qualified and successful migrants involves transfer of skills and knowledge, seen in cases where a number of return migrants have opened up businesses in their home countries. Especially since the 1990s, return migrants have remained highly mobile, making use of local conditions and often low production costs, and sometimes shuttling between homes in two different countries. These entrepreneurs make use of their transnational networks to connect with business partners in countries where they have spent many years and also their ties to other migrants in other countries with whom they share ethnic or national origin, migratory experiences, or university and professional education.

The success stories observed in a small number of countries have promoted the notion of brain gain and circulation for development. The role of highly skilled migrants in economic development in the communication and information technology sector is well documented, especially for some Asian countries, specifically China, Taiwan and India (Saxenian 2004). Overseas Chinese contribute between 60 and 65 per cent of all foreign investment in China and have thereby supported the necessary capitalization for economic growth. Even more successful has been the development based on transnational networks between Taiwan and industrialized countries, in particular the US. Many of Taiwan's transnational entrepreneurs had migrated for postgraduate studies to America, where they had remained and become successful engineers, managers and businessmen. When economic conditions in Taiwan started to improve in the late 1980s, a growing number of migrants returned and others began to commute between the two countries in order to make use of the business opportunities that had become available. Thus, two favourable conditions came together here, as in South Korea: the successful participation of migrants in prosperous economic sectors in the country of immigration alongside considerable economic development in the country of emigration and a number of migrants who were then willing to return or invest 'back home' given the new conditions. In fact, Taiwanese engineers had an important role, together with Chinese and Indians, in the success, first, of Silicon Valley and, later, other information technology sites in the US. Chinese and Taiwanese founded 20 per cent of all new companies in the Silicon Valley region in the second half of the 1990s (Hunger 2003), while returnees from the US established a greater part of the new companies in their countries of origin (Saxenian 2004). These strategies were generously supported by the respective states searching to benefit from the acquired knowledge and networks of their citizens abroad.

These are prime examples of how transnational groups and states contributed jointly to technological development and economic growth in these countries and successfully reversed the earlier brain drain (Saxenian 2004). In the case of India, however, the state was less prominent. Some authors also maintain that NRIs (non-resident Indians) have contributed to a positive image of India abroad but have brought about little impetus for economic development (Khadria 2002). Among other factors, Indians have returned in fewer numbers than Taiwanese or Chinese migrants (Saxenian 2004). The role of those who did return, however, seems comparatively strong. Twenty of the most successful Indian software companies, with a market share of 40 per cent of the sector, were established by return migrants. Almost all other companies in that sector have returned NRIs in their top management (Hunger 2003). Emigration of highly skilled people also affects many other countries, but the issue has not attracted the same interest everywhere from researchers and policy-makers. Tertiary-educated Mexicans, for instance, constituted around 14 per cent of all Mexicans (of at least twenty-five years of age) in the US in 2000. The proportion of highly qualified individuals abroad in relation to the total number of Mexicans holding a university degree is 10 per cent – considerably higher than that of migrants with university education from India or China (both around 3 per cent) (Hunger 2003; Tejada Guerrero and Bolay 2005). Thus far, most of the Mexican government's development initiatives focused on attracting transnational resources have concentrated on remittances. Since 2005, however, the Mexican government has aimed to promote ties between Mexico and highly quali-fied nationals living abroad in the business and education sector through the Mexican Talent Network (Newland and Tanaka 2010).

Especially since the 1990s, scientists have also contributed to the exchange and transfer of technology through so-called dias-pora knowledge networks (Meyer 2001). The emergence and recognition of scientific diasporas is related to four factors: the significant increase of highly skilled migrants from a particular country, facilitating interaction and network building; the evo-lution of new communication technologies and above all the Internet; the emergence of the knowledge society as an expression of the social and economic role of knowledge, information and education in contemporary society; and the sense of belonging of many expatriates to both their country of origin and their new country, and thus the existence of transnational identifications and formations (ibid.). The two best-known examples of scientific diaspora networks are the Colombian Red Caldas and the South African Network of Skills Abroad (Meyer 2011). The strength of these networks is based on the exchange of information and communication, the organization of scientific gatherings and con-ferences, and policy advising. Some have been short-lived, though, and several networks, such as the Red Caldas, dissolved after several years of active operation.

In spite of a number of successful strategies of involvement of migrants in knowledge circulation, brain drain still constitutes an important concern for many countries (Hamilton and Yau 2004). The World Bank's *Migration and Remittances Factbook 2011* (World Bank 2011) offers an impressive picture of the global map of highly skilled migration. For instance, in the year 2000, 97.5 per cent of all nationally trained physicians on the island of Grenada emigrated, together with a quarter of those trained in Somalia and Ethiopia – figures that severely affect the health-care system in those countries.

Different solutions to the problem of brain drain have already been developed. Some seek to follow the example of the Philippines, which, in response to the global demand for medical personnel, started to train more nurses than were needed for its national economy. Some destination countries have agreed to ethical codes of conduct which ensure they act responsibly vis-à-vis the labour demand in the countries of origin. Such codes include ways to compensate countries of emigration for the training and educational investment made (Stilwell et al. 2004). Other proposals are to expand dual citizenship in order to allow for the temporary return of settled migrants, rather than permitting migrants to stay only on a temporary basis and then return permanently. This could be a focal point for North–South cooperation, supporting migrants to engage in the development of their countries of origin. Dual citizenship could also be a means to foster South–South cooperation through collaboration between migrants from various Southern countries residing in developed countries of the North. Collaboration between Indian-American and Chinese-American migrants would be an example (Khadria 2009).

Social remittances and their effects

The implications of transnationalization for development are most frequently discussed with a focus on financial remittances and now more recently with respect to the potential for the circulation of knowledge for economic growth. Social remittances – ideas, norms and behaviours – are another form of cross-border exchange in which migrants engage. These have the capacity to contribute to social transformation within the family or local community and may promote political change, human rights, democracy and peace-building on a broader scale (Levitt 1998; Goldring 2004). For example, migrants who have experienced higher sanitary and health standards abroad have introduced new practices in their home villages, such as safe drinking water or keeping animals out of living spaces, and brought new ideas for environmental protection and waste management (Levitt 1998; UNDP 2009). Another outcome resulting from the cross-border exchange of norms and ideas about the distribution of household tasks is changes in gender roles and, generally, the claim for more equality between men and women (Levitt 1998, 2001a). We have already discussed these socio-cultural practices in chapter 2 and will recall their meaning only briefly for the development debate where they are now also discussed.

The outcome of the transfer of social remittances can consist in a more equal distribution of household work or of childcare within the family, as in situations where women specifically are no longer willing to accept a subordinate role. Such transfers may, however, just as equally cause conflicts within families and devalue the family as a whole (Levitt 2011). Extensive consumerism may result when both ideas about the Western (American) way of life associated with accessible consumer goods and the financial resources to purchase them are transferred. When young people in less prosperous world regions await a monthly cheque from their parents abroad and the day when they too will migrate, rather than making the effort to acquire an education and take a job, local economic development will suffer. Moreover, the transfer of resources does not benefit all family members equally and therefore may contribute to intra-family inequality – between sons and daughters, for instance (Amelina 2011).

The transnational practices of migrants also target democratization and political transformation in their countries of origin

(Smith and Bakker 2005: 133). Freedom of expression and democratic and liberal values experienced in countries of immigration encourage migrants to make demands on political elites and institutions in their home countries and towns. The new strength they have often gained vis-à-vis the authorities through their financial commitment to community development allows migrants to have influence and bargaining power in this respect. This has been observed in Mexico and some other Latin American countries, for instance, where the implementation and institutional control of democratic norms, the public awareness and fight against clientelist practices, and recurrent claims for human and (indigenous) minority rights have become significant in political debates through the influence of migrants (Laguerre 1998; Rivera-Salgado 1999; Smith and Bakker 2005; see also chapter 6).

Acquired attitudes can inform various practices as regards involvement in the country of emigration. Here, the wish both to aid infrastructure development and to contribute to social change and political awareness may not run in parallel. A study of Kurdish HTAs in Denmark, for example, reveals two different perspectives among the various associations investigated (Christiansen 2008). Some community leaders were eager to help and support development in their home villages, to raise money to this end and to engage in community projects 'back home'. Others, though, held a more hands-off position and were willing rather to support and inform those in the country of emigration about practices of accountability and the presentation of lawful demands before the state. While one group values the transfer of financial remittances, invests in the hometown and openly acts as development agent, a second group exemplifies a 'willingness to teach villagers how to get help from the state' (ibid.: 99), showing a more active stance on social and political remittances.

Yet, the involvement of transnational communities and diaspora groups for political change is not always positive (Shain 1999; Van Hear 2011). Diaspora groups contribute to the financing and fuelling of conflict by supporting combatant parties and the persistent sense of discord among those in their countries of origin. A comparative study of seventy-eight major civil conflicts between 1960 and 1999 worldwide has in fact found that the existence of a large diaspora abroad enhances the likelihood of violent conflict (Collier and Hoeffler 2002). In recent years, though, the potential of diaspora groups for the promotion of peace and support for reconstruction and democracy in postwar societies is encountered more frequently, with diasporas seen as peace-builders (Van Hear 2011). This implies that 'diaspora' can hardly be considered a homogeneous entity, and certainly not all transnational practices lead to peace and democracy. In fact, research presents a mixed and ambivalent picture in this regard, involving both positive and negative consequences and not always what was originally intended by the actors (ibid.). As with social remittances more generally (Levitt 1998: 944), neither the content nor the effect of transnational involvements is necessarily 'good'. Hence, the cross-border transfer of resources can provide sustainable income, ameliorate poverty and even contribute to economic growth. It can also deepen social inequality and serve to finance violent conflict. Whether judged 'good' or 'bad', transnationalization is today one of the key processes to keep in mind when exploring the nature of economic, social or political developments.

The effects of financial and social remittances depend *inter alia* on the experiences and living conditions available to immigrants. Whether the latter had the chance to learn about and experience new forms of gender equality or civic and political engagement in the country of immigration will influence the likelihood and content of such transfers. The role of migrants' transnationality for kinship networks, business circles and the development of home villages and countries depends upon the opportunities for participation and integration in the immigration state. From the angle of integration, transnational ties and practices are sometimes seen as more critical if not incompatible with the progressive adaptation of immigrants to their new homes. We will learn more about the relationship between transnationality and integration in the next chapter.

5

Transnationality and the Models of Migrant Integration

Transnationalization introduces a new perspective and a new area of study into research on international migration. In so doing it also challenges the existing models of migrant integration. The transnational approach shifts the focus from concerns about the dynamics of migration, the origins of immigrants, and the latter's adaptation to and integration into their new country towards the continuing ties migrants maintain across borders connecting the societies of both origin and immigration. From its very beginnings, the transnational perspective has signified a critique of the ideal of migrants' exclusive integration into the country of immigration and, as a consequence, of classical assimilation theory. Simply put, assimilation holds that those who arrive in a new country, often from very distant places (and in the case of the US not infrequently from across the ocean), and who bring with them different cultures, habits and languages, become part of that new society and thus integrated into its key institutions. While, at first, newcomers might experience some conflict when establishing new social relations and possibly face psychological difficulties in their process of adaptation, according to the classical formulation of Robert Park (1928) and, following him, the concepts of many other authors (Warner and Srole 1947; Gordon 1964; Alba and Nee 2003), they soon enter into contact with the new society and its members, accommodate to new habits, situations and people, and – provided that they do not meet with strong discrimination – eventually assimilate. In a stylized version of assimilation,

88

progressive cultural and structural adaptation is portrayed as an almost inevitable process that takes several generations, with eventual assimilation its final outcome. In the course of that process migrants would leave their old roots behind. The second generation in particular is expected to have few ties to the former homes of their immigrant parents.

Scholars advocating a transnational perspective have extended the focus from the country of immigration to include the emigration side and the fact that migrants do not necessarily uproot themselves from their old society. Rather, they are simultaneously embedded in both their new and their old homes (Glick Schiller et al. 1992b, 1994). They settle and integrate into their new country and at the same time remain engaged, concerned and affected by events in their country of emigration. Yet, the relationship between migrants' transnational involvements and their integration has remained a hotly debated issue. Critiques of the approach have questioned the possibility that migrants can be seriously involved with two societies and polities simultaneously. Indeed, this doubt has thus far been one of the main reasons why dual citizenship is rejected in many countries. National citizenship is meant to bind people to one polity, and one alone. Generally speaking, the objection is as follows:

the more transnational or multifocal ties migrants entertain, the greater their ambivalence towards the immigration polity, the weaker the roots in the nation-state of settlement, the stronger the incentives to form a transnational community, the bolder the claim to a diaspora, the greater the tendency on the part of the natives to question the allegiance of the newcomers, and, finally, the weaker the inclination to adapt in the country of destination. (Faist 2000a: 242)

For many scholars as well as policy stakeholders, transnational ties and successful integration may exist in parallel for some members of socio-economic elites and highly mobile classes who control sufficient resources to this end. But the majority of migrants are expected to integrate successfully into one society and one country exclusively, or to fail in all respects.

In this chapter, we elaborate on the ways in which transnationalization and migrants' transnationality challenge the concepts and models of migrant integration. We discuss four issues. The first two sections examine whether transnationalization and integration are mutually exclusive processes or whether they are complementary and interrelated. Some scholars have argued that assimilation may have been an adequate concept for the earlier nineteenth- and twentieth-century waves of immigration to the US, but it no longer holds true for migration dynamics in the twenty-first century. Therefore the next section highlights the view that transnationalization and the formation of transnational communities today create a new model of integration for an increasing number of migrants that has replaced older models. This perspective is based upon the existence of cross-border ties and resulting simultaneous engagements in more than one place. Other authors have noted that transnational migrants, or migrants involved in transnational spaces, are also exposed to the country of immigration and are therefore likely to adapt in some way. These authors argue that the processes of integration and transnationalization can also be regarded as interrelated. Therefore in the following section we shift to a perspective that sustains that transnationalization and integration are two different but interrelated processes which vary in their outcome for individuals and groups.

Whether or not transnationality is a new integration experience or simply one part of current processes of integration, the focus has been mostly on the first generation of migrants. Key to the understanding of integration processes, however, is the path these processes take over several generations. Therefore the third section of the chapter asks whether second-generation children of migrants also display intense transnational ties to the parents' old home and whether the intergenerational process of integration still takes place to the detriment of transnational ties and practices. Finally, although assimilation theories and integration models generally focus on the individual migrant, the formation of migrant associations has also received attention in this literature. We saw in chapter 4 that a growing number of such associations engage with the economic and political development of hometowns and countries of origin. From a simple assimilation perspective, it might be suspected that these transnationally active organizations divert migrants' efforts to integrate. From a transnational perspective, scholars have argued that migrant organizations frequently display a multifaceted character and are often engaged both 'here' and 'there' simultaneously. Thus, here again, the relationship between integration and transnationalization is described as either contradictory or interrelated. This is what we look at in the last part of the chapter.

Transnationalism as a model of integration

When the term emerged, 'transnationalism' was conceptualized as a different model of integration and a new paradigm for integration theories. It embodied a critique of classical assimilation theories, but also of ethnic pluralism. Because both of those models of migrant integration neglect or reject the relevance of cross-border ties, researchers objected that they could not adequately describe the new phenomenon of transnationalization which was increasingly characteristic of migrants' lives (Glick Schiller et al. 1994; Faist 2000a). The image so far maintained that people would move from their old homes to a new country and adapt to the new society, which would thus become their new home. Transient migrants would return to their old homes after temporary absence and were therefore not expected to adapt (Glick Schiller et al. 1994). The transnational perspective holds that many migrants settle and integrate into the new society and maintain cross-border ties and networks with their old homes simultaneously. This simultaneity became an important aspect of the criticism of existing models of integration at the end of the twentieth century (Faist 2000a). Against this background, the critique called into question the bounded conceptualizations of social ties and society, ethnicity and nationalism which had thus far predominated in migration research and social science more broadly, as well as in popular thinking and public debate. We discuss the epistemological implications and the methodological challenges resulting from this critique in chapter 7. Here we concentrate on its meaning for the models of integration.

The two main models of migrant integration which have dominated the discussion are assimilation and ethnic pluralism. The classical formulation of assimilation presupposes that identification, contact and activities would gradually orient migrants towards the place of reception following their physical relocation. They would learn to adapt to the language and culture of the mainstream society, and, although they often entered the labour market at the lower end and encountered discrimination, the expectation was that they would be moving gradually towards the core society and its key institutions. In the very elaborate version of Gordon's typology (1964), assimilation is a complex process of stages, starting with cultural adaptation (termed acculturation), followed by structural, marital and identificational assimilation, and, absent prejudice and discrimination from the mainstream society, leading eventually to civic assimilation – that is, the disappearance of deeper conflicts as regards values and power relations. Whether the newcomers adapt fully to the existing dominant culture (the Anglo-conformity model) or rather meld together with the existing societal core leading to a new mainstream culture (the melting-pot model), the relative homogeneity and exclusivity of social and political engagements and the fixation on one place is the outcome of this process. Ethnic differences would vanish or at least become insignificant for social contacts and structural integration after several generations born in the country of immigration (Warner and Srole 1947; Gordon 1964).

The term 'assimilation' emerged in parallel with the great wave of immigration to the US at the end of the nineteenth century, and its theoretical concepts were intended to describe this wave (Kivisto 2005). Indeed, for the vast majority of the descendants of migrants who arrived from Europe in the nineteenth and early twentieth century, ethnic distinctions have by now eroded; the job opportunities open to them are in principle equal to those open to other Americans; many have realized upward mobility, especially when compared to the lower-class position of their parents; cultural differences have diminished, along with the languages spoken by the first generation; and residential mixture and intermarriage have occurred over the generations. These migrants overwhelmingly identify as Americans (Alba and Nee 2003). While it is a widely shared perspective that assimilation has been the governing trend among those who arrived in these early waves of mass immigration, it is more controversial whether the same is true for new immigration in both the US and Europe.

New immigration in the second half of the twentieth century is generally considered to be different from that of earlier waves, more varied and impacted by different contexts and conditions (Alba and Nee 2003). Differences, especially concerning immigration into the US, include the fact that most new immigrants are not from Europe and are therefore considered culturally and racially less similar to the American mainstream. Because of their generally greater distinctiveness with respect to skin colour, racism and discrimination emerge as obstacles to assimilation. The other main difference is that job opportunities and labour market insertion processes have changed fundamentally. While earlier migrants encountered a flourishing and expanding economy which allowed the vast majority to realize their dream of a better life, new immigrants are confronted with a more fragmented situation. Mobility patterns have become more varied and there has been generally less job security. In this situation, whether assimilation is still a major trend has become more contested, and a second important model of integration has become subject to debate.

This other model of integration, which aims at conceptualizing post-migratory processes, is ethnic or cultural pluralism. Rather than presupposing cultural adaptation and homogenization, proponents of ethnic pluralism suggested that immigrant institutions would remain based upon distinct cultures (Kallen 1996). Migrants' integration, although of a more heterogeneous type than the one suggested by classical assimilation, benefits in this model from ethnic identification and ties. Migrants cultivate the heritage of their ancestors and maintain specific cultural traits, food habits and religious beliefs. Ethnic enclaves and their small-scale enterprises offer migrants job opportunities and options for upward mobility. The Chinatowns and the Little Italys of American cities are the real-world manifestations of this perspective. Based on their observation of this heterogeneity, scholars argued for the need to look 'beyond the melting pot' (Glazer and Moynihan 1963), and pointed to the fact that ethnic groups still existed, both in self-description and in external attribution. Rather than upholding static cultures and inflexible ethnic identifications, however, their cultures, habits and interests had transformed through interaction with American society. The logical question posed in this case was: What in modern America are new immigrants assimilating to? (ibid.).

In the 1970s, the ethnic pluralist model and the debate it generated contributed to a reconceptualization of the concept of assimilation and a critique of 'straight-line assimilation' as a uniform, linear and intergenerational process. Ethnic retention and the revival of ethnic identities have been described as 'symbolic ethnicity' (Gans 1979). This form of ethnicity, especially relevant for third and fourth generations, is expressed mainly in food habits, the consumption of symbols and the celebration of 'traditional' festivals and dress while integration into important institutions of mainstream society occurs. In addition, authors have stressed the non-linear character of this process as a 'bumpy-line approach' to assimilation (Gans 1992), one that recognizes variations in the adaptation processes of migrants. However, neither model – assimilation or ethnic pluralism – takes into account the continued relevance of cross-border linkages for migrants' lives and practices.

Emerging in the 1990s, the transnational perspective, in turn, has highlighted the cross-border expansion of social ties and spaces as a consequence of migration. Migrants in this view are not only connected to the place of their settlement, where they are in contact with mainstream and co-ethnic institutions, but also involved with their places of origin. They are, thus, connected to two places at the same time and maintain their lives within social spaces connecting two worlds. Much of the transnational literature suggests that migrants are today leading dual lives, with family and kinship networks on both sides of state borders, and over longer distances; that they participate in two or more polities; that they are culturally connected to multiple places; and that they have become economically active across borders (Faist 2000a). Transnationalization has thus been seen as a new form of integration distinct from the former two models. It is characterized specifically by the simultaneity of involvement.

Thus far, the scholarship on assimilation and that on transnationalization have been largely disconnected fields of inquiry, and the models of integration each of them favoured stood side by side. They are still most frequently dealt with separately. More recently there has emerged a slowly growing body of literature which investigates the relationship between the two processes of integration, or assimilation, into the society of the country of immigration and the transnationalization process or phenomenon which binds people to the place and community of their birth or ancestry (Morawska 2003; Kivisto 2005).

The relationship between transnationality and integration

The literature discussing the relationship between the transnationality of migrants and the process of their integration has opened a new field of inquiry. On the one hand, this research is interested in the importance of the phenomenon and asks how many migrants are affected by transnationality in their process of adaptation and whether those who are display characteristics different from those who are not engaged in transnational practices. On the other hand, empirical studies reveal many different combinations and variations of the processes of transnationalization and integration which report positive and negative results for the persons concerned.

Characterizing the transnational migrant

Thus, the first set of studies investigates the characteristics of the 'transnational migrant' in order to address the question whether transnationalization is a phenomenon that affects many migrants and whether such migrants are different from others. Is there 'a distinct class of immigrants' (Portes et al. 2002: 284) involved in transnational activities? Transnational studies on migrants' mobility and post-migration processes are based predominantly on qualitative, often ethnographic research. As a consequence, quantitative studies were needed to determine the extent of the phenomenon. In addition, as elaborated in the previous section, many scholars assumed that transnationality was likely an indication of an integration process that had not yet been successful or of withdrawal occurring on account of frustration and failure. Therefore it is important to ask whether these migrants are less integrated in the immigration society than others.

In addressing these questions, the Comparative Immigrant Entrepreneurship Project (CIEP) was the first to deliver quantitative data on the extent of transnationality, its association with particular characteristics among migrants in the US, and its linkages with the process of integration (Portes 2001; see also chapter 2, note 4). A first survey now also exists in the European context (Snel et al. 2006). The surveys include socio-demographic indicators such as gender, marital status, number of children and level of education, as well as factors related to integration such as length of stay in the country of immigration and citizenship status. Classical assimilation theory would predict that, in the course of settlement, identification with and orientation towards the country of immigration would increase while 'home'-country identification would lessen. Length of stay in the new country is therefore an important variable. Transnationality should be especially strong among recently arrived migrants, while those of longer residence should show little transnational orientation and activity. Other integration variables are holding the citizenship of the country of reception and the experience of social mobility upon arrival compared to that before migration. Migrants who experience serious downward mobility should be more likely to be transnationally active, since, for them, assimilation has not been an available option.

The CIEP data, which give an account of economic entrepreneurial activities as well as political and social-cultural engagements across borders, offer the following results (Portes et al. 2002). First, transnational migrants exist. The transnational entrepreneurs on whom the study concentrated comprise the self-employed or company owners whose business activities include travelling abroad and whose success depends on regular cross-border contact. These individuals comprise a distinct category of migrants, co-existing with wage workers and the domestically active self-employed. Second, this group is comparatively small, consisting of only 5 per cent of the total (representative) sample. Among the self-employed, though, transnational entrepreneurs make up 58 per cent. Third, neither recentness of arrival nor the experience of occupational failure shows a positive relationship with transnational practices. Rather, those of lengthier residence and in a socio-economically more established situation are more likely to be counted among the transnational entrepreneurs. This speaks against one of the most important expectations of classical assimilation, namely that successful integration would mean structural assimilation into the mainstream labour market, and not into ethnic and transnational niches. Thus,

> the data show that transnational entrepreneurs are better educated and more economically successful than either purely domestic entrepreneurs or wage workers. In addition, and contrary to what conventional assimilation theories would lead [us] to expect, results indicate that transnational entrepreneurs are more likely to be US citizens and to have resided in the country for longer periods of time than the sample average. (Portes 2001: 188)

The study identifies contextual factors which influence the extent and forms of transnationality among migrants. These factors are related mainly to the context of exit and reception. Where the specific historical situation of the origin context has promoted strong bonds of solidarity among migrants, migrants are more intensively engaged in transnational practices. In the CIEP study this case is represented by the Salvadorian informants, who have been characterized by strong bonds with their communities of origin since the civil war. After the return to peace and democracy, transnational social networks continued to exist and successful business activities developed out of these. In contrast, groups characterized by greater distrust among co-nationals in the country of emigration and, as a consequence, also in the country of immigration show fewer transnational entrepreneurial activities. These migrants can be found rather in salaried employment. This is the case with the Colombian interviewees, who share a more distanced relationship with their home country as a result of widespread violence and suspicion of involvement in the drugs trade.

Three different explanations have been offered for the relationship between transnationality and integration (Itzigsohn and Saucedo 2002). Transnational practices may simply be a continuation of ties which connect migrants to family and kin in the place of origin. Migrants may stay in touch with those they left behind, send remittances and travel home more or less frequently. This form is called 'linear transnationalism'. In this case, it is expected that such ties weaken over the course of time, as adaptation progresses and migrants become integrated into the immigration society. This scenario would be in line with the conventional assumptions of assimilation theories.

A second possibility exists when migrants want to maintain contact but cannot do so because they lack the resources to engage in intense cross-border exchanges. Newly arriving migrants often encounter difficult situations in finding work and getting ahead with their daily lives, so that they may not have the time or the financial means to travel home or send money. Once they progress economically, they may find it easier to engage in diverse kinds of transnational activities. When they achieve sufficient economic independence, migrants may even become transnational entrepreneurs. This is what is called 'resource dependent transnationalism'. In this case, integration precedes or parallels transnational activities.

The third form identified here emerges from frustrated efforts to progress and improve one's social status. Transnationality then becomes an option for improving one's prestige at least in the place of origin, through monetary contributions and the resulting recognition among kin and community 'back home'. In this

respect, migrants may also feel forced into transnational engagements in the face of discrimination in the country of immigration.
This form of transnationalism is considered 'reactive'. Its relationship with integration lies in the reaction to negative experience
resulting from marginalization and discrimination.

Using data from the CIEP, Itzigsohn and Saucedo (2002) have
tested these explanations and focused on socio-cultural practices
in order to investigate migrants' sense of belonging. The respective indicators included participation in hometown associations,
sending money for collective projects or participation in hometown festivities and other similar social and cultural activities.
What they discovered resembles the findings about transnational
entrepreneurs: people with longer residence in the United States
are more likely to participate in transnational cultural activities.
Further, return orientation has a positive impact on transnational
socio-cultural activities, thus supporting the assumption of linear
transnationalism, because people simply maintain contacts with
the place to which they wish to return. This is consistent with
assimilation theory. There was less support for the assumption
underlying resource-dependent transnationalism, since persons
with very few resources also participate in transnational spaces.
Here, only the data from the unemployed seem to confirm the
assumption that transnationalism follows after some degree of
integration. Experiences of discrimination and negative percep-
tions of the country of immigration, in turn, are also positively
associated with transnational engagements, underlying the reactive
transnationalism hypothesis.

A study of transnationality and its relationship to integration
undertaken among migrants in the Netherlands corroborates the
main results of the CIEP and also includes personal relations. On
a personal level, 'transnational activities occur equally among all
migrants, independent of the level of education, social status or
length of stay' (Snel et al. 2006: 294–5). Although the more public
form of transnationality – the transnational entrepreneurs – is rare
in that European country, the majority of migrants are involved in
other, more private kinds of transnational activity, mainly related
to family and friends. Transnational entrepreneurs, however, are

found more frequently among the more highly educated, thus lending support to the resource-dependent explanation that, in order to engage in transnational activities, a certain level of integration is required, at least for cross-border economic activities. On the other hand, while those more poorly integrated into the labour market are not more intensively engaged in transnational activities than the better established, they identify to a higher degree with the country of emigration. This again supports the finding that a certain level of resources is required in order to allow migrants to become transnationally active.

These findings, along with many other results which stem from the analysis of the data of the CIEP, show that transnationality is an important characteristic of current migration. Nevertheless, the degree to which migrants are transnational varies considerably, and some do not engage in transnational practices at all. In addition, transnational involvement varies across different spheres. Whereas only few transnational entrepreneurs seem to exist, at the level of socio-cultural engagement, and even more concerning family ties, a greater number of current migrants obviously qualify as transnational. Transnational ties do not disappear with longer periods of residence and progressive integration. Importantly, transnationalization is not incompatible with integration. Both processes can go hand in hand, and the better established and those with lengthier residence are more likely to be transnational, especially in the economic sphere. Still, reactive forms of transnationalization also exist. Marginalized migrants may direct their interests and identifications towards their community and country of emigration in face of limited integration opportunities and experiences of discrimination. Looking at these complex findings, it can be concluded that integration and transnationalization are not mutually exclusive processes. Rather they reflect two different aspects which can be related in different ways and with various degrees of success. However, in order to grasp these dynamics, a more open, less linear and static understanding of integration is required.

Combinations and variations of the integration–transnationalization linkage

Existing studies which disaggregate transnationality and integration along their different dimensions reveal rather selective combinations between the two processes. Scholars have noted in particular the differently combined variants across relevant social realms (economic, political, social and cultural). Integration here is conceptualized as a multidimensional, complex and not necessarily linear process (Levitt 2003; Morawska 2003; Kivisto 2005) tending to follow a 'bumpy line' (Gans 1992). Similarly, transnationalization is not a homogeneous process and 'the dimensions of transnational practices do not vary as a package' (Levitt 2003: 180). As a consequence, the relationship between integration and transnationalization is not uniform and may lead to different results in different social spheres. Levitt, for instance, suggests variations of transnationality with respect to movement, degree of institutionalization, scope, type and goal of activity (political, economic or religious, for example), and the socio-economic characteristics (class and stage in life) of the persons concerned. These different aspects combine in numerous ways among migrants:

> The migrant adult child who supports and cares for an aging parent via long distance or the migrant investor who receives daily reports from the manager of his farm or store are engaged in frequent cross-border contacts despite their limited movement. The believer who returns to her homeland only once a year but who consults weekly with her religious leader also participates in regular, patterned transnational activities. (Levitt 2003: 180)

At the same time that migrants are involved in transnational activities in ways that are meaningful to their lives, they are embedded in important ways in the country of immigration and thus subject to acculturation – that is, cultural exchange and adaptation – and potentially to assimilation. Individuals combine involvement with the country of origin and integration into the new country in different ways and with different degrees of success, related both to upward and downward mobility (see especially Levitt 2003; Morawska 2003).

Levitt relates three ideal-typical stories of varying combinations and success. Eduardo lived in the US and the Dominican Republic for several years with different members of his family but never managed to adapt to either society, and he feels unfamiliar with both of them; overall he is socially and economically marginalized in both settings. Thomas, in turn, is the paradigmatic case of a highly successful US-born child of immigrant parents who realized considerable upward mobility. At some point in life he became interested in and increasingly attracted by his parents' former home – Ireland. At this stage, he travels regularly to Ireland, where he is now engaged in several community projects. Pratika and Deepa are an Indian-born couple living in the US, whose economic success arises from resources in both America and India. Family ties and religious belief and habits tie them to India. The individuals in all three cases follow different paths in the combination of transnationalization and integration, with different degrees of success, as they assimilate to different segments of the immigration society. Hence, what these studies clearly illustrate is that the concepts of integration (or assimilation) and transnationality do not refer to the same thing. Assimilation focuses on integration into the country of immigration, while transnationality is concerned with the cross-border ties of migrants, in general to the country of emigration. The combination of both is manifold and the consequences vary greatly.

Second-generation transnationality

One of the main critiques made by assimilation theorists against the relevance of transnationality has been that this was only a first-generation phenomenon, and as such had always existed, while over time, and especially with the children of migrants born in the country of immigration, such ties would vanish (Fouron and Glick Schiller 2001: 64; Alba and Nee 2003). Thus, since full assimilation is expected to occur over several generations, the 'real' question of the importance of transnationality focuses on the second, and sometimes the third, generation. Is there something like 'second-generation transnationalism' (Jones-Correa 2002)?

Referring to the second generation, however, already raises some problems, and these multiply when viewed from a transnational perspective (Fouron and Glick Schiller 2001; King and Christou 2010b). The second generation is generally defined as those children of migrants born in the country of immigration or having migrated below a certain age, usually six years – that is, before school age (Thomson and Crul 2007). Sometimes the threshold is at the age of twelve (Portes and Rumbaut 2001), while in other definitions children born abroad but accompanying their parents in migration are considered the 1.5 generation (see chapter 3). Things become more complicated when parents have different nationalities or origins, and especially when one of them was born in the country of immigration while the other is a first-generation migrant. Moreover, migrants' children are not infrequently sent 'back home' to live with family and kin while parents are trying to move ahead in the new country. In the case of Eduardo (Levitt 2003), for example, his father, Diómedes, left the Dominican Republic for Boston before he was born, leaving his pregnant wife, Marcela, behind. When Eduardo was only a few months old, Marcela received the desired visa for Boston; however, it did not include her son, so she left him with her mother and went to join her husband. By the time Eduardo arrived in the US five years later, his parents were divorced and his mother had remarried. Eduardo had difficulties in adjusting to the new environment in Boston and could not adapt at school, not least because of his poor proficiency in English, and after several years of limited progress his parents decided to send him back to live with his grandmother. After a few years his grandmother increasingly felt overburdened with the youngster, and he returned to Boston. At the age of eighteen Eduardo had already been back and forth five times.

In other cases children of migrants may never join their parents but live with other family members in the hope that their parents will soon return – a current reality explored by transnational family research (Hondagneu-Sotelo and Avila 1997) in which new forms of parenting across borders can be observed (see chapter 2). As a consequence, the second generation has very diverse experiences. For example, among Haitian parents in the US there are those who 'have children born in Haiti who are brought to the United States only when they are teens, children born in the United States after their parents migrated but sent home to be raised in Haiti, and children born and reared in the United States. Consequently, households contain children with many different degrees of knowledge about Haiti' (Fouron and Glick Schiller 2001: 64) and with very different experiences of US society. Moreover, in today's increasingly dense cross-border spaces, other children and young adults, not necessarily children of migrants but perhaps their nieces and nephews, are involved in transnational social spaces, participate in communication across borders in their daily lives, maintain meaningful contact with family members abroad, and spend their leisure time with cousins returning to their parents' village for long summer vacations. These young people have therefore also been considered part of a 'transnational second generation' (Glick Schiller and Fouron 1999).

Does this imply that the second-generation children of migrants are transnational in the same way and to the same degree as their parents? No definite answer to this question exists as yet, but it seems rather unlikely. The second generation born and raised in their parents' country of immigration definitely has other experiences, is more exposed to that society, and is generally acculturated to it in some way. Still, the transnational experiences and identities of migrant children are a distinct reality today, along and sometimes interwoven with more segmented paths of assimilation than those conceptualized within classical assimilation theory (Portes and Zhou 1993). Even the return of second generations – that is, their independent migration to the country of origin of their parents – is now a social reality under empirical scrutiny. This is not least because countries of emigration call upon the loyalties and skills of migrant communities abroad to support development back home, through remittances and investment and by giving descendants of their (former) nationals preferential treatment within labour recruitment schemes. Japan, for instance, specifically targeted second- and third-generation descendants of those who had migrated to Brazil and other Latin American countries in the first half of the twentieth century with the purpose of attracting them to fill shortages in the Japanese labour market, especially in the 1980s and 1990s (Tsuda 2003). Around 250,000 Brazilian Japanese responded to this opportunity. These, in turn, started to re-create their Brazilian identity and lifestyle ever more strongly in response to their inability to conform to Japanese cultural standards.

The second generation's 'return' migration is often closely linked to transnationalization through ties and visits both prior to and after their migration, through continuous cross-border ties now flowing in both directions. Their return may, however, bring an end to transnational ties and close the circle of migration (King and Christou 2010a). Hence, the second generation may integrate into the country of immigration and maintain either very weak transnational ties or none at all. It is not unlikely that this is the majority. Children of migrants can also return to their parents' former homes and integrate there, with no wish to remain engaged with the place of their birth. From the existing literature on this phenomenon it can be concluded that this pertains to a very small number of people. Some migrant children, however, will maintain transnational ties and practices, although the meaning and content of these are likely to be different from those of the first generation. And since transnational social spaces (relationships and networks) involve people who may not themselves be transnationally active, the children of migrants exclusively integrated into one place are at least *potentially* transnational (Jones-Correa 2002). Some of them may (re)activate transnational ties over the course of their lives or in times of crisis, whether personal or political. In that sense, children of migrants are different from non-migrants. At the same time, some non-migrants, even those not connected to migrants, are transnational today (Mau 2007), and some similarities are likely to exist between children of migrants and non-migrants in maintaining cross-border contacts or in feeling attached to distant places. An important difference remains: for the first group, these transnational attachments are triggered by the migration experience of the parents and the place of their emigration, while, for the second group, transnationality is embedded in other types of experiences, global media, world risks and evolving cosmopolitan ideas, about which even less is known.

Migrant associations as a means of integration and transnationalization

Associations formed by migrants are another important focus of the literature on integration and transnationalization. They play an important role in the transnationalization of civil society, which will be discussed in chapter 8. Yet, such associations are also considered relevant means of integration. Immigrant and ethnic associations, today often more generically called migrant organizations, ease integration, since they fulfil relevant functions such as social support and basic orientation in the new society, give advice, and help find jobs through their networks or organize leisure-time activities and religious services (Moya 2005). Some scholars have highlighted their role as ethnic institutions contributing to integration and cohesion within the ethnic community rather than within the mainstream society in the country of immigration (Breton 1964). The greater part of the research today underscores their bridging functions in spite of the fact that migrant associations are generally an expression of ethnic identity formation. In the ethnic pluralist or multiculturalist perspective, migrant organizations are also welcomed as forms of institutionalization of cultural diversity and today are often supported as welfare agents (Jenkins 1988; Fauser 2012). A seemingly growing number of associations founded by migrants are also transnationally engaged with their home villages (see chapters 4 and 8). While drawing on migrants' attachment to the home country, these organizations were originally expected to foster attachment to the country of immigration, since their operation would inevitably draw them into exchange with institutions in the latter (Layton-Henry 1990). Yet, many migrant organizations are in fact multifaceted and multifocal (Cordero-Guzmán 2005; Fauser 2012). A comparison between locally operating and transnational migrant organizations in selected American cities revealed that the latter were almost as involved with local institutions as the former (Portes et al. 2008). Thus, one can find in these organizations plans for development in places of emigration at the same time as agendas for integration in immigration societies. What is more, migrant groups and associations lobby on behalf of human and minority rights on both sides of the border. Such activity has included cases as diverse as indigenous rights movements operating between the US and Mexico (Rivera-Salgado 1999) and Kurdish activism in Germany, in Turkey and on a European scale (Østergaard-Nielsen 2003b). Scholars taking a transnational perspective have argued, therefore, that integration and transnationalization are interrelated processes not only at the level of the individual but also at the associational level (Østergaard-Nielsen 2003b; Smith 2007; Portes et al. 2008).

In the age of globalization, one-sided perspectives focusing on what occurs in only one place are too narrow if we are to understand relevant social processes and core sociological concepts such as the family, cultural identification, political involvement or social inequality, along with the multiple forms of integration. The classical notion of assimilation, which describes a process running from cultural adaptation to the new society to structural integration into relevant mainstream institutions, paralleled by the lessening of attachments to 'old roots', has been challenged by the transnational perspective. From this perspective, the border-crossing expansion of social spaces has been revealed, and it has been shown that the processes of integration and transnationalization can not only co-exist but are often closely intertwined. Needless to say, not all migrants are engaged in the two processes, and those who are vary in the degree of their involvement in each as well as in the ways they combine both forms of involvement. While for some individuals and groups this combination yields successful results, for others it contributes to marginalization. Further research is required to determine more precisely and in greater depth the conditions and mechanisms which contribute to either outcome. The variety of combinations shows that transnationality is not merely one element in the pluralization of life courses and events; transnationality itself exists in a plurality of forms. The contributions of a transnational perspective lie not so much in introducing a new model of integration in place of older ones. Rather, taking transnationalization into account generates new insights and reveals more complex dynamics than had ever been considered by either assimilation theories or cultural and ethnic pluralism models. A transnational perspective again leads to the question, posed in the mid-1960s: 'integrating into what?' The paths of integration are more varied today and include upward or downward mobility and marginalization. Modern societies are ever more plural in culture and lifestyle, and many people deliberately subscribe to multiple identities. Cross-border engagements may even tie them to multiple locations. Understanding these processes and their interplay is crucial to understanding people's lives and social transformation in the twenty-first century.

6

States and Citizens – Transnational Political Practices and Institutions

While markets and families can very easily be thought of in cross-border ways, this is not the case with states and citizens. In much of normative political theory, and in empirical social research, the relationship between states and citizens is conceptualized as if the political activities of citizens were necessarily contained only within the territorial confines of their respective nation-states. Cross-border transactions in the political sphere are often relegated to specific fields of theorizing and research, such as diaspora studies. Yet migrants' cross-border practices have been a regular feature of political life for more than a century and raise crucial questions about membership in states of both immigration and emigration. Consider those migrants who have a stake in two states. Over the past decades, states have increasingly come to tolerate the right of migrants to carry two passports, one from their country of origin and the other from the country of immigration. They possess dual citizenship. But this leads to questions such as: Are dual citizens loyal to both the country of immigration and the country of emigration? Are they allowed to exercise their rights, such as the right to vote, in both states? How do emigration states try to maintain links to their (former) citizens living abroad, and through what kinds of policies? In what ways do such policies contribute to migrants' transnationality? Dual citizenship is thus an ideal site for the exploration of the social and political practices of individuals, groups and organizations across borders, on the one hand, and the changing political institutions of national membership in immigration, emigration and countries of onward migration, on the other.

There is a duality of political institutions and political practices: political institutions provide opportunities for transnational political practices, while the practices contribute to the transformation of political institutions. Citizenship is one of the basic institutions of contemporary polities. Political practices beyond the borders of nationally bounded polities challenge the congruence of full membership within the trinity of one territorial state, one people and one state authority (Faist 2004b: 331–2). Political institutions are usually demarcated by territorial and membership boundaries. Political practices can be juxtaposed, as transnational practices take place in networks and social spaces transgressing the container of the state.

A transnational perspective looks at the web of transactions across the borders of nation-states. As an analytical perspective, a transnational approach accounts for both transborder nationalism and nation-transcending conceptions of political community and membership, without being committed to either of the two. Transnational practices include forms of cross-border participation in the politics of both emigration and immigration states. There are three types of cross-border political transactions. First, migrants may become involved directly in the politics of their regions of origin. Second, they may become involved in the affairs of their countries of origin via the political institutions of the country of immigration (Østergaard-Nielsen 2003a: 763). Third, they may seek to participate in the politics in the country of immigration by appealing to their country of emigration – for example, through consular bodies. In all of these instances, political participation in one country, such as voting or lobbying, is informed by political events in another.

The following analysis suggests how the changing boundaries of citizenship – as expressed in the growing toleration of dual citizenship and cross-border political practices – are a challenge to a state membership no longer restricted by territorial borders, one state authority and one people within those boundaries. First, this chapter examines the concept of citizenship and its three main dimensions – equal political liberty and democracy, the rights and duties of both citizens and states, and affiliation to a collective, often conceptualized as a nation. Second, the discussion continues by looking at the changing policies of dual citizenship towards a higher degree of toleration. This part focuses on countries of immigration and international organizations, since they have been driving this change. This is not to say that countries of emigration are not important players in the changing policies of dual citizenship. Yet they have usually followed the legal changes in the countries of immigration. Third, the chapter turns to the politics of citizenship and thus to an analysis of transnationality. The focus here is on the political practices of collective actors, such as diasporas, with respect to democratization and nation-state-building.

Citizenship: a conceptual sketch

Citizenship is a contested and a normative concept (Walzer 1989), and today refers most often to full membership in a nation-state. There are no authoritative definitions. According to the Aristotelian tradition, citizenship constitutes an expression of full membership of persons in a political community, with the objective of equal political liberty, irrespective of whether the citizens are governing or governed (see Aristotle 1962: III.1274b32–1275b21). Citizenship is important both as a legal concept – legal citizenship or nationality (*nacionalidad, nationalité, Staatsangehörigkeit*) – and as a political concept. As a political concept, it has three main elements – equal political liberty, rights and duties, and collective affiliation.

As a legal concept, citizenship denotes full membership in a state and the concomitant ties to state law and subjection to state power. The interstate function of nationality is to define a people within a clearly delineated territory and to protect them against the outside, at times hostile, world. The intra-state function of nationality is to define the rights and duties of members. According to the principle of *domaine reservé* – exclusive competence – each state decides within the limits of self-determination on the criteria required for access to its citizenship. One general condition for membership is that nationals have some kind of close tie to the respective state, a 'genuine link'.

In contrast, viewed as a contested political concept, citizenship concerns the relationship between the state and democracy: 'Without a state, there can be no citizenship; without citizenship, there can be no democracy' (Linz and Stepan 1996: 28). In essence, citizenship builds on collective self-determination – that is, democracy – and essentially comprises three mutually qualifying elements: first, the legally guaranteed status of equal political freedom and self-determination; second, equal rights and obligations of all full members; and, third, affiliation with a political community.

1 Equal political liberty: Citizenship relates to the principle of democratic legitimation with respect to the acceptance of rule and the process of rule-making. Flowing from this first and basic dimension are citizenship practices – the ways in which relations between citizens and the political community as a whole unfold over time and, more specifically, how citizens negotiate and shape their citizenship. Ideally, citizens endowed with equal political liberty obey the laws in whose creation they have participated and to whose validity they thus consent. Without such democratic procedures to guide their political self-determination, citizens would be little more than subjects of a state sovereign.

Certain challenges for the first element, democracy, may arise in cross-border situations. Citizenship is bounded, while transnational political practices, such as external voting or collective lobbying (from abroad), cross state boundaries. The substantive challenge for democracy lies in the pluralization of membership – for example, dual citizenship – and multiple status positions – for example, citizenship in one country and the status of alien (temporary resident) or denizen (permanent resident) in another. Denizens are mobile individuals who, as emigrants, remain citizens of their country of origin and, as immigrants, are permanent residents without full political rights in their country of settlement. Dual citizens, in principle, have rights to vote in two countries, but does this violate the basic democratic principle of 'one person, one vote'? And is it normatively acceptable that people live in their new country for many years without being granted the right to vote? With a perspective on countries of emigration, on a more empirical level, the questions are whether and in what ways trans-national political practices contribute to the democratization of states or whether they strengthen authoritarian rule.

2 Rights and duties: The legal aspect of citizenship guarantees the right to nationality and other rights associated with it. In general, citizens' rights fall into various realms: civil rights to liberty, such as due process (the right to fair court proceedings); rights of political participation, such as the right to vote and to associate; and social rights, including the right to social benefits in case of sickness, unemployment and old age, and the right to education (Marshall [1950] 1964). Various extensions to this classical triad have been discussed, prominent among them the cultural rights of minorities (Kymlicka 1995). Among the corresponding duties are to serve in the armed forces, to pay taxes, to acknowledge the rights and liberties of other citizens, and to accept the democratically legitimated decisions of the majority.

Should non-resident citizens be allowed to vote in local or national elections in their country of origin? Conversely, should non-citizen residents be allowed to vote in elections in their countries of immigration? In both respects a sea change has occurred in recent decades. An increasing number of emigration states provide voting rights to emigrants. As to the second question, there are in principle two answers. One is to allow non-citizen residents from outside the EU to have local voting rights, which is exactly what an increasing number of European states have done. The other is to facilitate the naturalization of permanent residents. One instrument with implications for cross-border political participation is dual citizenship, which has been seen to increase the willingness of immigrants to take up citizenship in the country of immigration (Faist 2007). However, the question remains as to whether emigrants should remain loyal to their country of origin.

3 Collective Affiliation: Citizenship implies affiliation to a political community, often understood as the 'nation'. Citizenship rests on an affinity of citizens with certain political communities and loyalty to a self-governing collective. Such collectives claim to establish a balance between individual and common interests, on the one hand, and the rights and responsibilities within the political community, on the other. Affiliation with a collective, whether a nation or another entity, expressed as a set of relatively continuous, social and symbolic ties among citizens otherwise unknown to one another, is linked to the second element of citizenship, because there exist reciprocal obligations of members in a political community, akin to a social contract.

Several questions arise in this context: Are diasporic communities which lobby for regime change in their countries of origin more often fuelling violent conflicts – as was held by many observers to be the case with the Tamil Tigers in Sri Lanka – or are they more likely to act as agents of democratization – as was the case of South African expatriates at the end of the Apartheid regime? After all, we should also consider collective agents in the discussion of citizenship. Political institutions and practices matter not only at the individual level but also at the collective level, as the practices of diasporas, transnational communities, transnationally active migrant organizations and the national state attest.

The policies of citizenship: the case of dual citizenship

Citizenship across much of the world over the last two centuries has been a fundamental status involved in the drawing of boundaries – that is, inclusion in and exclusion from membership of persons and groups. We now consider how and why the policies of various states have changed towards a greater toleration of dual citizenship. A transnational perspective seeks an understanding of the mechanisms by which the boundaries of full membership in states are (re)drawn, so that overlapping membership is countenanced. In this section we look at the politics of citizenship in the transactions between the states concerned, using the case of Germany and Turkey. What we see emerging is a not altogether new form of transnational citizenship, above and beyond citizenship in nation-states, but a multiple membership, such as dual citizenship. This is more properly the transnationalization of (national) citizenship – in other words, national citizenship jumping onto a transnational track.

Germany and Turkey are examples of states that are linked to each other through transnational social spaces and which react to each other's membership policy changes. In the early 1990s, arson attacks in the German towns of Mölln and Solingen killed eight Turkish women and girls. In the belief that Turks in Germany would be fully protected only if they had German citizenship, the Turkish government reacted by changing its previous policy of discouraging naturalization in Germany. At the same time, Turkey wanted to strengthen its links to its largest expatriate community. In 1995, it introduced a 'pink card' that facilitated renunciation of Turkish citizenship by guaranteeing former Turkish citizens most of the rights they had previously enjoyed, though it did not provide for the franchise in Turkey. Turkish migrants apparently did not trust the value of this external quasi-citizenship. A substantial number of migrants renounced their Turkish citizenship only temporarily in order to become naturalized in Germany, but then reacquired it through the Turkish consulates. The Turkish authorities colluded, thus exploiting a legal loophole that, before 2000, had not permitted the German authorities to deprive German citizens of their nationality while they resided in Germany. In 1999, the new red–green coalition government in Germany, made up of the Social Democratic Party and the Greens, promised to introduce reform to promote dual citizenship, but failed to implement this crucial element of its proposal. The new citizenship law that came into force in 2000 stated that applicants for naturalization should renounce their existing nationality. Shortly before the regional and federal elections in 2005, the German authorities deprived about 20,000 immigrants of Turkish origin of their German citizenship because they had reacquired Turkish nationality, arguing that they had violated the rules governing citizenship in Germany. This episode illustrates how states whose citizenship regimes have become entangled in rather densely knotted transnational spaces may act independently to pursue their own political goals, but still become exposed to the policy choices of the other. In the end, the German government, against the opposition of Turkey, decided to uphold, in principle, the rather restrictive renunciation clause. This occurred not despite but perhaps because other citizenship rules were liberalized at the same time.

The German–Turkish case illustrates the dynamics of agency. The larger historical context of dual citizenship helps us to identify the principal mechanisms underlying the political dynamics just described. In the past, including the recent past, policy-makers considered dual citizenship a problem. Leading politicians of previous centuries saw it as contrary to the natural order, the equivalent of bigamy. Citizenship and political loyalty to the state were considered inseparable, hence plural loyalties were unthinkable. The Hague Convention on Nationality (1930) stipulated that 'every person should have a nationality and one nationality only' (quoted in Faist 2007). Policy-makers worried that dual citizens would not integrate in the host country and would maintain exclusive loyalty to the country of original citizenship. And, in times of war in the nineteenth and early twentieth centuries, they feared 'foreign' interference by citizens belonging to enemy states. Moreover, democratic legitimacy was at stake. Policy-makers feared that dual citizenship would violate the principle of 'one person, one vote', while diplomats pointed out that they could not protect the newly naturalized citizen in their original country. Yet over the last few decades an astonishing change has taken place: an increasing number of governments regard dual citizenship not as an insurmountable problem for integration, foreign policy and diplomatic protection, but as a challenge that needs to be negotiated from standpoints ranging from (mostly) pragmatic tolerance to active encouragement. More than half of all the states in the world, countries of immigration as well as emigration, now permit some form or element of dual citizenship (see figure 6.1). Even in countries that do not as a rule accept dual citizenship, such as Germany, Denmark and Iceland, because of rules allowing for exceptions, the number and percentage of dual citizens have been steadily growing.

Figure 6.1 Dual citizenship around the world

Source: Faist (2010a).

The growing toleration of dual citizenship has been brought about above all by changes in family and gender law. In general, the changes have been slow. Sometimes path-dependent developments in international law have filtered down, and are embraced but also resisted by national states. Legal norms on statelessness and gender equity have acted as a lock-in mechanism, tying liberal-democratic nation-states to universal norms, and the Convention on the Reduction of Statelessness of 1961 is now adhered to by all liberal democracies. With respect to gender equity, among others, the Convention on the Nationality of Married Women of 1957, the UN Convention on the Elimination of All Forms of Discrimination against Women of 1979 and the European Convention on Nationality of 1997 have been incorporated into national law. At the national level, lobby groups have worked hard to implement international conventions. In Germany, for example, the 'Association of Women Married to Foreign Men' engaged in effective pressure-group politics in the 1970s and 1980s. Ultimately, as a result of the conventions, the activities of pressure groups, and national laws, women do not lose their citizenship upon marriage to a man of another nationality, and children from binational marriages are entitled to dual citizenship.

There has also been a second type of path-dependent mechanism, namely a disincentive effect. In many European countries national courts have strengthened the rights of non-citizen residents since the 1960s. On the supranational level within the EU, the principle of reciprocity among member states has led many states to strike out the renunciation clause when citizens of other member states naturalize. Countries of emigration have followed the lead of immigration countries, and have increasingly used dual citizenship as a means to connect with their citizens abroad, now often collectively referred to as diasporas. Nonetheless, increased toleration of dual citizenship has been a bumpy road, sometimes followed by new restrictions (Faist 2007).

Governments of nation-states in general have used citizenship as a mechanism of social closure to distinguish between members and non-members. The emergence of aliens with partial membership rights – so-called denizens – has posed a new challenge to dual citizenship, since admittance to full membership could come either from easing access or from increasing rights short of full legal membership. Allowing dual citizenship, when countries of immigration make it easier to retain original citizenship – naturalization without renunciation – is obviously an example of the former. One prominent argument to rationalize this kind of liberalization has been to promote the social integration of immigrants through ensuring the congruence of the voting population (demos) and the resident population. This central argument has always rested uneasily with the rights of emigrant citizens, where the 'genuine link' between citizen and state is more tenuous. In countries of immigration, immigrants 'inside' and emigrant citizens 'outside' were even weighed against one another, as in the Netherlands and Sweden. For example, in cases where emigrants enjoyed dual citizenship, those who advocated multiple citizenship for immigrants argued that fairness demanded that both emigrant citizens abroad and immigrants should enjoy dual status.

Countries with significant proportions of emigrants have subsequently also adapted their citizenship laws in the direction of greater tolerance of dual citizenship among their citizens abroad. The case of dual citizens in diasporas is an interesting one. Migration usually implies only geographical exit and not a permanent loss of membership in formations such as kinship systems or states. This idea has become more influential over the past decades and may have contributed to a transition from regarding emigrants as 'traitors' to seeing them as 'heroes'. A prominent example is the People's Republic of China, which has changed its policies since the late 1970s. Its slogan to 'serve the country' was replaced by the motto 'return to serve'.

Adaptation of the legislation and practices of countries of emigration to the rules of countries of immigration has reinforced the spread of toleration of dual citizenship. It eases day-to-day interactions between governments and emigrants abroad. Although governments may still distrust the loyalty of (some of) their emigrants, toleration has the advantage of joining the ever-increasing international credo of mobility as a resource for development, as evidenced since the early 2000s by the (former)

Global Commission on International Migration and the policies of the World Bank. In the view of these international organizations, migration has mutated from a problem signalling underdevelopment to being part of a solution to what is called development (see chapter 4).

The cognitive mechanism of symbolic recognition is a prime example of how the tension between transnational ties and political institutions has been addressed. First, many migrants commonly have attachments and involvements in two or more places across national state borders, and consequently they have plural identifications and loyalties. When dual citizens regard their citizenship as an essential part of their identity, they often express emotional difficulties deciding which citizenship they would keep if they had to give up one of them. The toleration of dual citizenship may recognize the specific symbolic and emotional cross-border ties immigrants have (see chapter 2). Socio-cultural transnational activities of immigrants can reinforce their self-images and collective solidarities. In these cases, they regard the respective state's acceptance of dual citizenship as a kind of official legitimation of their pluri-cultural identity (Pitkänen and Kalekin-Fishman 2007). Second, the attachment or even loyalty to the country of immigration of children of migrants is facilitated if the respective state accepts or even embraces dual citizenship. This is mainly because the self-confidence in developing specific competencies related to a transnational background, such as bilingualism and intercultural role-taking, is encouraged as a result. In Germany, for example, those who have been dual citizens since birth – children of binational marriages – regard dual citizenship as important for their process of social integration (Schröter and Jäger 2007).

Dual citizenship has been discussed here as an example of a national institution where the boundaries of political membership have become more permeable to allow eventually for its compatibility with transnational ties. With increasing tolerance towards dual citizenship, national citizenship has become 'transnational citizenship' (Bauböck 1994). While in principle the character of citizenship as a mechanism of social closure has not changed, its boundaries have been altered and the tension between transnational ties and national institutions is less strained – which is not to claim that such liberalization would not be irreversible in times of war and intense interstate conflict.

The politics of citizenship: citizens, diasporas and states

Access to and the practices of citizenship are an important requirement for the exercise of voice in democratic states. The previous section dealt with the changing policies of citizenship which enable such access. It is now time to explore how the substance of citizenship as a national institution is impacted by transnational practices and how (national) political institutions in turn shape transnational practices of cross-border agents such as migrants. The focus therefore is on how cross-border citizenship practices are mutually constituted by states and politically active non-state agents. Since citizenship is not simply about state–citizen relations but also about reciprocity and solidarity among citizens, the analysis also probes issues of collective agency – for example, social relations within diasporas.

Before delving into an analysis of transnational politics and institutions, it is necessary to reflect upon a crucial term which has experienced a revival, this time as a transnational agent – diaspora (see also chapter 3). The term 'diaspora' has a very chequered history. Originally used to describe the dispersal of Jews after the destruction of the Second Temple in Jerusalem, the concept later referred to minority situations of religious communities, until it came to describe mostly ethnic (or ethno-religious) and national minorities abroad. In this way it differs crucially from notions such as transnational networks. Diaspora, as a concept used by political activists and analysed by social scientists, usually revolves around a specific set of markers, normally ethnicity and/or nationality. By emphasizing ethnicity or nationality, political activists occlude other markers involved in social practices, such as transnationality, gender, sexual orientation or legal status. Also relevant for our purposes is how researchers deal with this process. When they simply follow the claims made by political activists, they fall into the trap of the one-dimensional characterization of migrants as members of ethnic and national groups, while migrants may also be adherents of religious communities, sports clubs and professional associations – all potentially relevant for politics. We may thus think of diaspora more usefully not as a bounded political and cultural community but as a political claim (Brubaker 2005: 12). Nonetheless, this insight should not lead us only to deconstruct the discursive uses of diaspora (see Dufoix 2008) but to inquire into the conditions for mobilization across borders and the impact of successful claims on citizenship.

In the recent past, the term diaspora has resurfaced to describe collectives of emigrants or dispersed people who conceive of themselves or are conceived of as living away from their (ancestral and/or imagined) homeland, having not assimilated culturally, and pursuing a political or religious project. The term these days is often invoked by nationalist groups speaking for such imagined collectives and trying to push nation-building or by governments tapping into the resources of 'their' emigrants abroad, controlling them or protecting ethnic minorities living in another state. Recently, source countries of migration have also used 'diaspora' to encourage financial investments and promote political loyalty among economically successful expatriates. In general, it is helpful to understand diaspora as the contingent outcome of political mobilizations within transnational social spaces. It is important to realize the consequences of diaspora claims for central political institutions involved along the three elements of citizenship sketched above: equal political liberty and thus democratization; rights and duties; and collective affiliation.

Equal political liberty

All immigrants are at the same time emigrants. While research of the 1980s and 1990s focused on the role of emigrants, and in particular diasporas, in fuelling conflicts in their homelands, current research and policy debates emphasize their role as mediators in violent conflicts, as post-conflict developers and as agents of democratization. This change in emphasis is paralleled by a change in geopolitical constellations. Until the end of the Cold War, diasporas and the superpowers used one another to interfere in the internal affairs of emigration states. South–North constellations were thus an integral part both of the East–West conflict and of the aftermath of decolonization, which involved nation-building projects in the former European colonies. When the Cold War ended, diasporas had to search for new fields of activity, and development cooperation surfaced as one of them (chapter 4). Development has been broadly understood by leading international donors and institutions as implying primarily economic development, yet to be complemented by the institutionalization of the rule of law and democracy. Set in this frame of reference, the discussion on diasporas has included not only financial remittances but increasingly also a focus on migrants as agents of social remittances. The term thus also refers to migrants who maintain affective and strategic relations back home while engaging with and adapting to the country of immigration. These migrants are thought to have the potential to transform politics in their country of origin via 'ideas of citizen rights and responsibilities and different histories of political practice' (Levitt 1997: 517) which they observe and practise in the immigration state. These social remittances are then sent home and shared with significant others. This link helps to direct our attention to the first dimension of citizenship, equal political liberty. This dimension can be examined at the level of individual migrants and at the collective level.

At the level of the individual, there is some empirical evidence from the Mexican–US transnational space to show that international migrants may engage as agents of democratic diffusion who help strengthen democracy in their countries of origin (Pérez-Armendáriz and Crow 2010: 120). Return migrants have shown higher rates of non-electoral political participation, greater tolerance of political and social difference, and more critical evaluations of democracy and observance of rights in Mexico. More specifically, the data suggest that, on average, the attitudes of return migrants are more democratic than those of their co-citizens who have no type of migration experience. Yet their political participation in the country of origin might be restricted because they tend to be stigmatized as individuals who failed abroad. Among those who stayed home, the strongest migration-driven diffusion effects obtain among people who receive information directly from migrant friends and family who remain abroad (ibid.: 141). The implications of the study are useful because they challenge arguments that migration prevents democratization merely by serving as an escape valve in the case of those most likely to seek to transform the political system. At the very least, even if temporary exit serves as a safety valve, these migrants may mobilize abroad for change in their countries of origin and thus constitute a challenge to authoritarian rulers.

Once we move our level of analysis from the individual to the collective, and thus go beyond the attitudes of individual (return) migrants and their dependants, the available empirical evidence suggests a more mixed picture. In their study of migrant transnational politics and democratization processes in the Dominican Republic and El Salvador, Itzigsohn and Villacrés (2008) found that migrant transnational political practices in these two countries have been strengthening formal democratic rules of organizing political competition. Their analysis also shows, however, that the contribution of migrant transnational politics to the deepening of democracy is limited. In detail, the authors show that migration from both countries started as a result of authoritarianism, political repression and the absence of socio-economic opportunities. Through exit, migrants formed a new constituency to be reckoned with by the rulers in the countries of emigration. Nonetheless, there are clear limits to how migrant transnational politics contributes to the deepening of democracy. In the Dominican case, low rates of participation of (return) migrants, and the fact that the right to vote is seen by most as a symbolic right, diminish the impact of the migrant vote and confine it to those who work within the established party apparatuses. In the Salvadoran case, hometown associations (HTAs) have contributed to the emergence of participatory institutions and to the dynamism of local political participation. Beyond these channels, migrants have become a new and unaccountable power group. They may use their resources to impose their own agendas on non-migrants – namely, those who have to live with the consequences of development projects (see also Waldinger et al. 2008). We should thus be cautious about casting migrants as agents of profound political and social transformation. After all, in some instances migrants are themselves members of local elites, although diaspora groups may radically challenge existing political regimes. Also, we should not forget that the interests of migrants are most often focused more strongly on participation in the politics of the immigration state.

Nonetheless, there is evidence from other cases that diasporas do play a role as 'agents of democratization', especially in the post-communist world of Eastern and South-Eastern Europe (Koinova 2010). These are cases when diasporas are involved with democratization efforts rather than nationalist agendas. If, for example, the Ukrainian, Serbian, Albanian and Armenian diasporas are linked to states that enjoy both international and domestic sovereignty, they may focus on substantive elements of democracy, such as the extensive political participation of citizens. Although diasporas were not the most likely agents of democratization in the post-communist world, they have nevertheless made a contribution.

There is a curious absence of literature on the effects migrants have on democracy in countries of immigration. On the contrary, some normatively inspired literature deals with the threats of immigrants to Western democracies (e.g., Huntington 2003 on Mexican-Americans in the US). There is no systematic evidence supporting this notion, and most of the discourse is a portrayal of fears associated with the growing presence and visibility of people of Mexican origin in the US and Muslim groups in Europe (see also Faist and Ulbricht 2013).

Diaspora organizations certainly are influenced by and often skilfully employ global meta-norms of 'a nation for each people', democracy, human rights and gender equality – and yet remain embedded in local discourses. All of this also raises the question of how consequential diaspora politics and the extension of citizenship rights across borders of nation-states actually are, and in what ways they may contribute to the ongoing transformation of citizenship. In emigration states it is exceedingly difficult, as the discussion on democratization has suggested, to measure how much influence transnationally active associations and networks can exercise (Østergaard-Nielsen 2003b). Moreover, it is hard to evaluate the claims of representativeness not only for diasporas as a whole but also for individual migrant associations. The most we can ascertain is that they somehow represent immigrants who try to exert influence from the country of immigration into the home country context. There are no formal mechanisms of accountability. Even more important, evidence of legitimacy based on political substance or content is often hard to garner.

One of the important questions for countries of immigration is whether engagement in the country of emigration is incompatible with the political integration of immigrants. In a nutshell, the question is whether 'in between' means 'neither here nor there' or 'here and there', albeit to varying degrees in the different locales. Several scholars in the past have argued that migrants' organizations are crucial in fostering their political incorporation into the immigration state (Rex et al. 1987). Yet, few studies have systematically analysed the role of migrants' organizations in promoting that dual process of sustaining political action both 'here and there' as a simultaneous venture – simultaneity being one of the main characteristics of transnationality (see chapter 2). The findings from a study on migrant associations in Barcelona, Madrid and Murcia suggest that transnational engagement is by no means universal among migrant organizations in Spanish cities. Yet, a majority of them are engaged in some form of transnational linkage (Morales and Jorba 2010). Transnational activities even seem to foster overall political incorporation into the Spanish body politic, and this is especially the case for the more politically oriented type of transnational links (see also chapter 5). In sum, the two orientations, the integration of migrants into immigration states and their engagement in regions of emigration, do not constitute a zero-sum game but could actually mutually reinforce each other.

Rights and duties – states reaching out to emigrants

Democracy as we know it is institutionalized in some form of statehood and national states have become dominant in forging citizenship. Nation-states sometimes also cater to the interests of emigrants to use them for their own purposes. Countries of origin have over the most recent decades rediscovered diaspora politics and policies as a means to tie the 'global' to the 'nation' and rhetorically to elevate migrants from 'traitors' into 'heroes'. 'The emigration state' (Gamlen 2008) is therefore an integral part of the social constitution of extra-territorial groups via various mechanisms.

One may also view the regulation of rights and duties of emigrants as an effort by emigration states at their (re)integration into the country of origin through various public policies. Some states have referenced their emigrants in statute – for example, to 'maintain concern' for citizens abroad and foster their contacts with the homeland (Slovenia). Of prime importance is the recognition of diasporas, expressed in extended consular services – there are, for example, about fifty Mexican consulates in the US, as well as the Institute for Mexicans Abroad. Some states complement such measures by trying to sustain national cultural activities abroad via the distribution or broadcasting of national television and state-sponsored web portals. In tangible ways states sometimes even establish new migrant associations, such as 'Amicales' in the case of Morocco, or 'Diaspora Knowledge Networks' in the case of South Africa and Colombia (Meyer 2011). One of the purposes of such policies is to control a loyal diaspora and to include citizens abroad within a national community (cf. Bauböck 2003).

There are various forms of the extension of rights to emigrants:

- *Access to and renewal of citizenship*: This covers repatriation of citizens, the restoration of citizenship, preferential naturalization and (un)restricted dual citizenship. In connection with the latter, some states offer their emigrants dual citizenship with such restrictions ('citizenship light') as limits on voting rights, office-holding and property ownership of citizens living abroad. Other states offer more extensive citizenship (rights) for emigrants – for example, full voting rights from abroad. Nevertheless, practically all states have some cut-off point at which citizenship is not granted to the children of emigrants who do not entertain genuine links to the home country of their parents or grandparents.

- *Political rights*: Emigrants' political rights encompass external voting (abroad) or even special political representation in national assemblies, as is the case in Italy (Lafleur 2011). As a matter of fact, most countries allow for the electoral participation of emigrants in some form. The most widespread rule is that they must return to their district of origin to vote, although more and more states allow their emigrants to vote from abroad. There does not appear to be a link with other non-political interests: countries with proportionally large diasporas and remittance flows are no more likely to permit extra-territorial voting than others.

- *Social and civil rights*: Consular services are available also to protect the civil and human rights of emigrant citizens in their respective countries and ensure the transfer of social security benefits. The latter requires bilateral agreements, which are more common among European countries than in Africa or Asia. This state of affairs clearly signals that European citizens are better able to enjoy the portability of social rights. Consulates may provide special identity cards for non-resident nationals. For instance, the *matricula consular* (consular identification card) helps Mexicans in the US to open a bank account and to acquire a driver's licence. States such as Argentina, Colombia, El Salvador, Honduras, Peru, India, Morocco and Pakistan have similar cards. And the Philippines claims to protect the welfare of its emigrant workers, from recruitment to return, and even to intervene in labour disputes.

Underpinning political, social and civil rights are special measures taken by states to maintain the loyalty but also to reinforce the duties of emigrants. Prominent among these are mixtures of economic incentives, patriotic exhortations and marketing ploys, such as 'roots tourism' in Ghana. Also relevant here is the Mexican matching fund programme Tres por Uno (Three for One). More specifically, the following aspects can be differentiated:

- *Financial resources*: Some states also offer special incentives for emigrants to remain connected and in so doing tap into the specific resources available through migrants. Such policies include eased investment and taxation rules for emigrants (on India, see Kapur 2010). Other policies extend to pre-departure, return and integration programmes, practised in, for example, Ireland and Germany. Courting diaspora investments is particularly prominent, as in the case of the overseas Chinese for the People's Republic of China. A large percentage of foreign direct investment in China comes through investments by overseas Chinese. Similarly, though in a less spectacular way, Irish emigrants abroad contributed to the 'Celtic Tiger' boom of the 1990s. And Turkey, for example, offers expatriate-seeded venture capital funds (Dişbudak 2004). There is another side to such programmes: a few states have tried to levy taxes on emigrants – the US and Switzerland are among those who levy taxes on all expatriates. And sometimes the extraction of contributions occurs through less formal channels – for example, Eritrea's war-time 'healing tax' (Koser 2003). Yet more often states sign treaties with other states to avoid double-taxing.
- *Human resources*: It is not only monetary capital which is sought after by emigration states but also the resources embodied in highly skilled experts and scientists. These emigrants may be lured back to their country of origin, or at least remain tied to the emigration state through the aforementioned diaspora knowledge networks.
- *Policy advocacy*: Governments also see emigrants as foreign policy advocates in the respective countries of immigration. Historically successful cases, such as the Israeli and Irish emigrant lobbies, and nowadays also Arab emigrant lobbies, in Washington, DC, come to mind. In the eyes of some emigration

states emigrants are expected to act as ambassadors for their countries. Yet not all such countries are successful in engaging citizens abroad in homeland affairs.

Although the policies of emigration states have been listed according to categories such as the type of rights granted, it is striking that governments usually revert to a mix of programmes which seek to strengthen loyalty – that is, the sense of belonging to the state – and provide incentives to invest and return or circulate. In this way they thus aim to increase the desired forms of transnationality. Sponsoring participation through including emigrants into the populace and using them as a lobby group may sometimes be a goal. More often than not, however, emigrants' voices cannot be tightly controlled by their home state, as evidenced in the activities not only of separatist and irredentist diasporas but also of political opposition groups. Tapping into the financial and political resources of their emigrants, state governments may even foster unintended outcomes such as increased leverage of such groups 'back home'. In sum, there is by no means a one-way street of states extending public policies, such as citizenship rights, threats or surveillance; emigrant groups, too, participate actively through their practices in the making of the national state institutions, whose activities are directed at them.

Collective identity and nation-building

Understanding citizenship practices necessitates a look at the transactions not only between states and citizens but also among emigrant and immigrant citizens and other citizens. The subsequent analysis starts with emigrant citizens and includes those who are migrants with full membership status in the country of immigration but also those who are permanent residents or holders of temporary permits – or even undocumented ones. The transactions between collective non-state and state actors not only provide a good picture of socio-moral resources among citizen collectives, such as reciprocity, solidarity and trust, but also reveal the implications of membership.

Diaspora groups who represent themselves as ethno-national communities are a prominent type of collective transnational agent. Quite often they claim to deliver social remittances such as increased democratization, gender equity and human rights. Diaspora groups may also pursue claims for national self-determination. The claims coming from ethno-national groups are a particularly disputed phenomenon. Three categories of transnational groups in particular pose potential challenges to the country of emigration: refugees and exiles, stateless diasporas and state-based diasporas. The role of all three clearly goes far beyond the flow of financial capital, such as financing rebel armies (Collier and Hoeffler 2000), and has to do with the definition of interests and identities of political communities. States are not only established upon organizational infrastructure and various mechanisms of legitimate rule-making and rule implementation. They also rely on common elements of identity which underpin political communities such as nations. Membership in such communities is based on formal ties not only between states and citizens, but also on trust among the citizens themselves. Such trust among members in political communities cannot simply be created by states in a top-down process.

Refugees, émigrés and members of stateless diasporas often conceive of themselves as the vanguard of a new national state, or a national state to be reformed or revolutionized. At first sight they seem to be challengers or even competitors of existing (emigration) states. The transfer of politico-cultural capital takes various forms, ranging from the activities of exiles aimed at the improvement of human rights in their countries of origin to long-distance nationalism which strives to form a new nation-state. One of its critics, Lord Acton, called diasporas 'the nursery of nationality' (cited in Hockenos 2003: 262). Prominent examples include the roles played by refugee and exile communities that have fuelled conflicts in the countries of origin from abroad, such as Kosovo Albanians, the Mujahedin in the case of Iran and Chechen freedom fighters. A high degree of politico-cultural coherence can be found among 'stateless' diasporas whose declared intention is the founding of a new nation-state or at least achieving a high degree of autonomy in the declared homeland. Such communities are represented by organizations or liberation movements which are in clear conflict with the former homeland, as the cases of some Kurdish and Tamil communities attest (Van Hear 2011). Yet, by mediating between competing groups or providing resources for reconciliation and reconstruction, refugees and exiles have often had a significant impact on political development. Prominent examples are the South African diaspora's role in the anti-Apartheid movement and the more recent engagement of the Ugandan and Nigerian diasporas. In these cases, the rhetoric which accompanied political mobilization around transnational efforts has been good governance and rule of law, the implementation of human rights and democratization. Much less attention has been paid to the potential role of migrants and their children to resolve conflicts in the country of origin, such as in Afghanistan.

State-based and established diasporas, such as the Armenian, Chinese and Palestinian diasporas in the US and Europe, are considered by the homeland as strategic assets, as in the Chinese government's view of highly skilled overseas Chinese. The notion that homeland and diaspora constitute 'one people' is especially strong for relatively weak, new or reconstituted states, as well as for states in conflict with other states or groups (e.g., Armenian–Azeri groups; Shain and Barth 2003). One may argue that a national diaspora participating in the foreign affairs of the country in which they are domiciled ceases to be a disenfranchised group and becomes one with an entry ticket into mainstream society and politics (see Shain 1999 on diasporas in US foreign policy). Yet strong diasporas and fledgling home states produce a complex arrangement of international and transnational politics. Established diasporas may play a crucial role in the definition of national interest and national identity, both of which are best seen as flexible, rather than static, constructs. Forms of transnational identity may connect both homeland and host country. The interests of the diaspora and the home state may diverge significantly and are not a unified whole. There are instances of transnational identities of a nationalist kind, as in the case of Poland and Ireland and their diasporas which formed in the US during the nineteenth and the first part of the twentieth century. In exceptional cases, some interpretations of the transnational identity may be detached from a national identity and thus compete with statist transnationalism, as in the idea of a Jewish diaspora not centred on the state of Israel but in a global diaspora (Boyarin 1994). All of this suggests that transnational practices revolving around national interests can support, compete with or even challenge the congruence of a people, territory and authority in a state. One of the challenges goes beyond this trinity. If transnational groups conceive of themselves as diasporas connected to a nation-building project, such as Kosovar Albanians in the late 1990s, they usually portray themselves as ethnically homogeneous entities – in short, a *Volk* based more on a common cultural heritage than subjective predispositions of citizens towards a state and a constitution. The consequences of diaspora practices towards the fragmentation of existing (emigration) states are highest when the former pursue a *völkisch* orientation, which prioritizes nationalism as an ideology at the cost of other forms of solidarity. We could then speak of a form of nationalist transnationality.

Transnational citizenship?

The changing face of citizenship, its transnationalization in particular, is inextricably related to transnational practices of migrants and to the intensity and extensiveness of cross-border practices – transnationality. Dual citizenship implies a pluralization of memberships which overlap national states. It is the legal expression of the transnationalization of life worlds, well exemplified by migrants and their children. Although the transnational practices of migrants are not the prime cause of changing forms of citizenship, there has been a strong correspondence between transnational social and symbolic practices, on the one hand, and multiple, in this case, dual citizenship, on the other.

To what extent can we speak of transnational citizenship? Sceptics would argue that citizenship cannot be transnationalized in a fundamental sense (Turner 2001). In this view the term 'transnational citizenship' results in conceptual overstretching. While this criticism may apply to world citizenship, which is not institutionalized in a legal sense, there are forms of citizenship beyond that of nation-states, such as European Union citizenship (Faist 2001). Dual citizenship, however, is a form of transnational citizenship still tied to (multiple) national citizenship and thus not superseding it. What we see as a consequence of transnationalization in this case is not the demise of national citizenship, but a subtle change in its operation with far-reaching implications. Dual citizenship is an instance of a 'both/and' and not an exclusive 'either/or' membership.

7

Transnational Methodology

A transnational perspective on cross-border migration and its
consequences extends beyond the countries of immigration and
encompasses regions of both origin and destination, as well as
other places which are criss-crossed by the ties and practices of
persons, groups and organizations. Many of the research results
and insights presented in the previous chapters have been derived
by adapting known methodologies and methods to the needs
of a transnational optic. Based on the vast range of knowledge
generated by transnational studies in the field of migration, we
can now explore how these results were generated. This requires
a methodological toolbox for studying transnational phenomena empirically. Our endeavour here also includes a discussion
of how relevant research techniques are applied, using selected
examples.

Usually methodology is discussed in relation to a particular
discipline or an established field of research. Here it is the field of
migration from a transnational point of view. This consideration
of methodology is important for understanding the methods that
have been used to arrive in a systematic way at substantive results
regarding the topics of interest: the meaning of transnationality for
life chances; the genesis and reproduction of cross-border social
spaces; the implications of transnationalization for development
in the countries of emigration and immigration; the social integration of migrants; and the changing political practices, membership
and public policies of the states involved. In short, methodology

What is methodology?

connotes a set of procedures or methods used to conduct research. It provides a systematic basis for deciding which methods are likely to provide the types of knowledge needed to answer specific research questions.

Three methodological challenges for transnational analysis

methods for ethnography? transnational research

This chapter aims to define in more detail the methodological challenges for transnational research and to present adequate methodological tools. It gives an overview of methods used to tackle these three challenges and to analyse transnationality and processes in transnational social spaces. These methods are multi-sited ethnography – that is, fieldwork in various sites and places across countries; mobile ethnography – that is, the research conducted by the researcher en route, following the migrants; the extended case method, in which theoretical assumptions are defined from the start and followed by empirical work; network methodology, which helps to locate cross-border ties of individuals and collectives but also identifies virtual networks on the web; and quantitative surveys and longitudinal (panel) studies. Of these methods, most scholars working with a transnational lens have used multi-sited ethnography. The extended case study method, quantitative surveys and network methodology have been employed less frequently, and mobile ethnography (a very recent method) and longitudinal studies (which involves high costs in terms of time and funds) rarely. Thus, the results reported in the previous chapters have come mostly from multi-sited ethnography, and less often from quantitative surveys and studies using network methodology. There are three methodological challenges for contemporary migration studies in general and for transnational research in particular (for more extended expositions, see also Amelina et al. 2012; Amelina and Faist 2012).

Challenge no. 1: methodological nationalism

Immigration researchers too often presume the nation-state to be the (only) central relevant context for empirical studies on cross-border migration, as if the state were a container. State and society are held to be coterminous and territorially identical. There is the assumption that societal practices and national states and the collection of data within the confines of national states are congruent. In general, methodological nationalism in the social sciences marks the tendency to treat the container of the nation-state as a quasi-natural social and political configuration (Wimmer and Glick Schiller 2003, based on Martins 1974: 276). Primary examples of this assumption can be found above all in studies on migration control and the social integration of immigrants. Most of them deal with immigration regulation and immigrant integration in a single national state; at most, they compare regulations and social processes in various nation-states. Consequently, the organization of empirical research is limited to the territorial container of a nation-state, usually one that receives immigrants. We find this container thinking not only in older assimilation theories (Gordon 1964) but also in more recent conceptualizations. In a nutshell, most research has presupposed unquestioningly the congruence of society, the institutional arrangements of the nation-state and the related territorial framework – in other words, of people, state authority and territory.

Various authors have outlined the negative consequences of methodological nationalism in migration studies. Wimmer and Glick Schiller, in particular, differentiate three types of methodological nationalism. First, they argue that mainstream migration studies do not pay attention to nationalism and its effects on nation-building processes. According to the authors, sociology defines 'the limits of society as coterminous with the nation state, rarely questioning nationalist ideology embedded in such a founding assumption' (2003: 579). One pertinent example running against such an assumption consists of the efforts by nationalist diasporas to establish a national state of their own, in the past struggling against multinational empires, such as the

137

Austro-Hungarian or the Russian Empire, today against national states, as in the case of the Tamils and Palestinians. This is an instance of how nationalism as an ideology is guiding the practices of collective actors. Second, Wimmer and Glick Schiller criticize an understanding of nation-states as quasi-natural entities which neglects how they structure social relations. Such an understanding leads to a close coupling between national state authorities and social science, not only by funding programmes that support migration research, which are often governmental, but also by research which excludes all non-sedentary parts of the population. In quantitative research, for example, this has the effect of omitting from the picture such mobile individuals as seasonal workers or undocumented migrants. Third, the authors argue that empirical social research focuses primarily on the territorial boundaries of nation-states. But the 'territorial limitation' of power relations is a historically new phenomenon that emerged in the process of national state establishment, whereby the formation of nation-states itself was determined by cross-border power dynamics and activities. As a consequence, there has been a mismatch between cross-border phenomena, on the one hand, and the collection of statistics, on the other: 'The subject matter of international migration is cross-national in scope, whilst international migration statistics are the products of national government ministries, administrations and statistical institutes' (Singleton 1999: 156).

In sum, the assumption that the nation-state is the main social context of migration as well as the territorial framework of empirical migration studies determines both strategies of research design and methods of data collection and analysis (e.g., Bonifazi et al. 2008). Of course, this is not to argue that nation-states are not important for analysis. For specific research objectives, a focus on the nexus between state authority and territory is helpful – for example, in understanding immigration control. Over the past decades many immigration states have increased the efficiency of their border control and thus control over migrants (Faist and Ette 2007). Yet a sole emphasis on this congruence of state authority, territory and society is inadequate if researchers are to understand both how transnational social spaces emerge and are reproduced and how the practices of migrants and non-migrants are involved. The critique of methodological nationalism should not lead to the role of the nation-state being disregarded. The main point is not data collection on the national level but the missing attention to cross-border ties and their consequences. Therefore, it would be premature simply to replace the nation-state as the main unit of analysis with the household, the city or even the world.

Various alternatives to the nation-state as the quasi-natural unit of analysis have been proposed. Most prominently, these have involved the global network approach and world theories. Yet these also suffer from a major defect in that they define peremptorily and in advance a primary unit of analysis. The first of these privileges cross-border networks. The network approach to globalization (Castells 1996) describes and explains why and how social life has become 'disconnected' from territorial limitations in general and national state territories in particular. This view rejects the claim that society is congruent with the nation-state and its institutions but holds that it is made up of social networks criss-crossing the globe. The second position, the world systems approach (Wallerstein 1974), views the globe as a single overarching system. Despite significant differences between them – for example, relating to the role of the nation-state – both take a bird's-eye view, from the top down. They hold that the world view is a privileged vantage point. In particular, while the network approach eschews fixed categorizations and stresses the novelty of hybridity in a world of constant motion, it leaves unchallenged the notion that, in the past, ethnic and national identities were fixed. Also, in overgeneralizing de-territorialization, it overlooks processes of spatialized capital accumulation (Massey 2008) as well as the global restructuring of social spaces along the intensity, density and velocity of flows (Held et al. 1999). According to world systems theory, nation-states are crucial elements making up the centre, periphery and semi-periphery of a tiered political-economic global system. Although world systems theory reflects on nation-building as a historically specific process, it views spatiality and geographic mobility as predominantly unchanging physical properties that need not be considered when analysing social practices.

Therefore, we need to redefine the unit of analysis with care. One rule of thumb is to be very precise as to the scope of empirical analysis and reference to the respective collective. While the state could be a unit of analysis – for example, in public policies relating to diasporas – other units of analysis are possible, depending on the research question – for example, kinship groups, local communities and organizations, or transnational social spaces. For an alternative social context to the nation-state, transnational social spaces form an available conceptual tool which can serve as a point of departure. This requires scholars to reflect upon spatial concepts which are often implicitly applied in empirical analyses. We then assign to the respective social context a relationally organized spatial framework in looking at ties and practices – of which, as is evident, nation-states are an integral part, although only one of several possible parts. Nation-states, for example, control access to their territory by regulating flows across borders, by determining who is admitted to (full) membership, and by engaging in diaspora policies.

In sum, units of analysis need to be chosen according to the level(s) analysed: household, networks of people or organizations, (international) organizations, states or state-like structures, such as the European Union. Thus, instead of starting off with the national state and the system of nation-states or with a borderless world of networks, it may be more fruitful to use concepts such as social space to delineate the social formations relevant for the subject areas. To put it briefly: there is no privileged unit or site of analysis from a transnational point of view. A transnational methodology has to consider both de-territorialized elements, in the form of intense flows across state borders, and territorial elements in the efforts of states and organizations to control such flows and establish criteria of membership for individuals. An appropriate starting point is therefore the concept of transnational social spaces, which include both a 'space of flows' and a 'space of places' – the former referring to the de-territorialized and the latter to the territorial elements (Faist and Nergiz 2012).

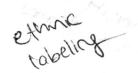

Challenge no. 2: essentialism

Quite often ethnicity or nationality is used unquestioningly as the dominant category relevant for research, and sometimes migrants are seen above all as members of an ethnic group – for example, Turks or Mexicans or Filipinos – and their roles as workers, professionals, parents, children, lovers, members of associations or local communities are not considered sufficiently. Thus an essentialist approach treats groups as quasi-homogeneous and does not consider the internal heterogeneity of migrant categories. It thus reproduces the primacy of the national or ethnic lens. To be more precise, the starting point for this type of research is how a particular ethnic or national group integrates or is incorporated into a national polity. Such an approach can also be found in studies on transnational practices. Consequently, many qualitative studies which dominate transnationally oriented research select interview partners according to their ethnicity or nationality. Yet it would be misleading to reject outright the use of ethnic and national categories as a way of entering the field. Rather, it is necessary to reflect upon their use and also to employ alternative categories, if appropriate and possible.

Categories such as 'Mexican' and 'American', or 'Turkish' and 'German', are frequently used as central criteria in research designs with no regard either to the ways in which these categories are formed by scientific and non-scientific discourses or to the conditions under which they are relevant for the social practices of mobile and non-mobile people. For this reason, researchers can benefit from reflecting upon the ethnic labelling of research designs, methods of data collection and data interpretation (Glick Schiller et al. 2006). One way to deal with essentialism is to build procedures of self-reflection into the design of the empirical study.

Migrant formations can be built around various categorical distinctions, such as ethnicity, race, gender, education, professional training, political affiliation and sexual preference. Ethnicity, in particular, constitutes a particularly vexed issue when using a transnational lens. On the one hand, it should be able to overcome the ethnic bias inherent in much migration scholarship. The fallacy

ethnicity's imp. is overstated

is to label migrants by ethnic or national categories. Often scholars presuppose prematurely that such categories matter a great deal for all purposes, since that is often the case in public discourse. On the other hand, by using the appropriate methods researchers should be able to trace actually existing social formations, such as networks of reciprocity built around ethnic markers, which are critically important, for example, in informal transfer systems of financial remittances. To do so requires treating the importance of ethnicity as an empirical question.

The use of an ethnic lens within the organization of empirical research is sometimes accompanied by naturalizing views on ethnicity. By defining ethnicity and nation as naturally given entities resulting from common cultural scripts, researchers consider neither the constructionist quality of 'group formation' nor the processes by which ethnic and national categories are socially developed, distributed and applied (Brubaker 2004). Researchers fall into this trap, which is especially relevant in the study of diasporic and transnational communities, if they do not probe into how such communities are socially constituted in processes of interaction with other groups. In committing this mistake, researchers accept that such communities are stable over time and are of overriding importance for the individual identities and social practices of their members. Researchers then do not consider that markers of difference other than ethnicity and nationality – such as transnationality, gender, class, religion or even lifestyle – may be equally as or even more important than ethnicity or nationality to group members. If they are not aware of this problem they may easily fall prey to nationalist propaganda promoted by both diasporas and governments. The two challenges of methodological nationalism and ethnic essentialism are closely related. Without overcoming essentialism we would simply replace nationalism with transnationalism – one -ism with another.

Under conditions of transnationalization, people may hold multiple memberships in different social spheres. To be more precise, they are able to hold different ethnic, national or religious affiliations simultaneously. This may even extend into the legal sphere. Take the example of multiple citizenship: there are more and more people around the globe who are citizens of more than one state. And, correspondingly, an increasing number of states no longer require renunciation (see chapter 6). This way of thinking about multiple attachments, memberships and roles is not novel, but rather involves the application of a fundamental sociological insight that individuals may engage in various, sometimes even conflicting social roles. Transnational methodology simply adds that such roles and belonging can extend across the borders of states – quite plausibly so, because societies are not bound by the territorial reach of states. In general, this way of thinking considers a 'both/and' logic of multiple memberships to delineate units of analysis. In this view, researchers broaden empirical procedures by refusing an 'either/or' logic of methodological nationalism.

This self-reflexive stance stimulates strategies of empirical studies, such as de-ethnicization (Fenton 2004), which build on constructivist and process understandings of ethnicity (Barth 1969). Heterogeneities other than ethnic or national belonging may be relevant for answering specific questions. In each instance it is necessary to pose the question: 'What is it a case of?' In other words, the significance of heterogeneities is determined by the question asked and should not focus peremptorily on ethnicity, just because we are dealing with migrants. In conducting empirical research on a particular ethnic group of immigrants, researchers can transcend the ethnic focus by avoiding premature assignment of common cultural traits and other commonalities to the category of migrants in question. For example, they can begin by focusing on other heterogeneities, such as religion, as an entry point (Glick Schiller et al. 2005).

Challenge no. 3: positionality in multi-sited research

Transnational analysis raises in a very urgent and obvious way the issue of the positionality of the researchers, an especially pertinent matter if research is carried out across states and researchers from both regions of imigration and emigration collaborate. Positionality here does not refer to the politicized or ethnicized position of the researcher(s) but looks at the context in which the methodology employed is situated. Multi-sited research entails not only inquiries in various sites in different countries but often also calls for the collaboration of researchers with respect to research design, data collection and interpretation. Problems arise over the asymmetry of control over social scientific concepts and funds which impact upon the relationships of those in transnationally composed research teams. For example, in most cases it is the researchers from immigration states, financed by their home states or supranational organizations such as the European Union, who control the funding. This puts researchers from states of origin – often non-OECD and non-EU countries in the East and the South – at a severe disadvantage, since they are often relegated to carrying out research designed by their Western and Northern colleagues. An even greater problem is the domination of scientific concepts and worldviews. As the history of sociology over the past decades suggests, most research and publications, as well as theory development, are produced in the metropoles of the West, and researchers in other parts of the world have difficulties bringing in their specific approaches. Although there is a long tradition of 'southern theory' (Connell 2009) in Africa, Latin America, India and other parts of Asia, most transnational research projects are dominated by scholars in the West. This gives rise to some well-known problems. For example, collaboration can sometimes lead to the mutual ethnicization of the collaborating researchers – in short, the individuals and institutions involved are also part of the respective transnational social space in which and upon which they have chosen to conduct research. The resources and, more generally, the power asymmetries between North and West, on the one hand, and South and East, on the other, are reflected in the design, conceptualization, operationalization, implementation and interpretation of empirical research across borders.

Positionality also concerns the position of the researcher vis-à-vis the research subjects. One may look at the boundary construction around identification, such as researcher versus worker, as situational 'boundary drawing' and 'boundary redrawing'. There is usually a complex configuration of the researcher's positionality from the optic of heterogeneities such as class and gender, in

hierarchies
between researcher and
researched

articulation with national identity. In particular, it is useful to
reflect upon power hierarchies between researched and researcher
along lines of gender, class or ethnicity. Such hierarchies emerge
in situations in which the two parties define their interactions by
using terms along various heterogeneities and assign each other
more or less powerful social positions. As ethnographic research
has long recognized, such hierarchies are not always clear-cut.
While some authors have argued that it is mainly the researchers
who have the power of definitions over the researched, because
they have the power to select empirical observations, questions
and results, the relationship within the research process may be
relational and changeable (Coffey 1996).

The inherently multidisciplinary transnational perspective helps
us to take up and extend the challenges posed to early migration research in the first two decades of the twentieth century.
A fitting historical example is the five-volume masterpiece *The
Polish Peasant in Europe and America*, by William Thomas and
Florian Znaniecki (1918–20). The authors devised concepts such
as 'super-territorial organization' (Vol. 5) in order to deal with
the role of migrant organizations in the US and their cross-border
links back to Poland. In the present day, the quantity and quality
of transnational linkages and associations may have increased not
only in this but in other cases. In fact, Thomas and Znaniecki can
themselves be considered to have been a transnational research
team. In addition to their work carried out in Chicago, both
scholars spent a considerable time in Europe: Florian Znaniecki
collected data in Poland and William Thomas conducted research
in Europe on and off for about ten years. Today research projects
often go well beyond the cooperation between two researchers,
and we must therefore think carefully about the prerequisites for
collaboration in larger research teams (Faist 2004a: 30–2).

Methods to address the three challenges

Transnational methodology is evolving to address the distinct
challenges of methodological nationalism, essentialism and

the positioning of researchers in transnational social spaces. Innovations in methods are necessary, and we are in the midst of an ongoing debate on how best to achieve them. While criticism of established methodologies is by now widespread, ways to overcome the three challenges have not yet been agreed upon. The most important task is to devise methods appropriate to the research question – that is, the case at hand.

To illustrate how the research question itself can guide the selection of the method we refer again to *The Polish Peasant*. The methodology the authors used clearly depended on the question they and in particular William Thomas posed – namely, how social 'disorganization', which was caused by modernization, could lead to a reorganization of the social order. He was preoccupied with how people were exposed to social change, and how this change was reflected in migration and settlement, both in Poland and in the US. While he took account of transnational ties, Thomas was nevertheless bound to the image of migrants as being 'uprooted' – quite distinct from metaphors used by later researchers – namely, 'transplanted' networks of immigrants and those engaged in 'translations', resulting in hybrid forms of 'both/ and' cultures (see chapter 1). To study the repercussions of what he perceived to be social disorganization, Thomas certainly could not rely on classical ethnographic methods, such as participant observation. While walking the streets of Chicago and pondering the problem, so the story goes, he was quite by accident nearly hit by a garbage bag – and out fell a letter written by a Polish peasant to a relative in Chicago. Subsequently, Thomas hit upon the idea of analysing letters to develop what later became biographical methods in sociology. The main point here is that there is thus an 'elective affinity' (Weber [1904] 1959) between theories and concepts, the main questions asked, methodology and methods used on the ground.

Today, nearly a hundred years later, a wide array of different methods is available in the research of cross-border practices and social spaces. There are even efforts to link qualitative and quantitative methods. Nonetheless, we need to consider that there are two different logics of research, exemplified by the two types of method. The quantitative approach, which often employs statistical procedures, seeks to estimate the effects of variables at various levels (people, countries, etc.). For example, researchers may ask what effects the transnationality of migrants and their associated households may have on the educational opportunities of children. Data are collected on a range of different variables indicating transnationality, such as visits, stays abroad, exchange of goods and information, but also on the educational background and professional position of parents and the frequency of shifts from one educational system to another. Based on this information, it is possible to estimate how much of the variance is accounted for by the different variables identified. In essence, quantitatively oriented research measures the average effects of variables. By contrast, the aim of qualitative approaches is to ask questions about the properties of a case and seek to account for the particular outcomes in a particular case. In the example just used, the interest might be why the result of shifting children of parents with comparable socio-economic backgrounds from one country to another might be different. Instead of identifying only which variables account for the difference, qualitative research asks 'how' questions: How have the agents involved interpreted their experiences? In which ways have processes led to the differential outcomes observed? It is important to emphasize that research in both quantitative and qualitative realms may seek to account for mechanisms which lead from an initial condition – in this case, moving children of parents with similar socio-economic backgrounds – to different outcomes – in this case, differences in educational success. So, while mixed methods occupy an increasingly prominent role, especially in survey studies, we should be aware that the logics themselves cannot be mixed.

Multi-sited ethnography, mobile ethnography and global ethnography

One of the earliest and most widespread forms of research into transnational formations is ethnography in various sites of the borders of states. The starting point is identifying the actual

follow the movements of the subjects of study

empirical field by tracing the ties and practices across borders. The basic principle of multi-sited ethnography, as suggested by Marcus (1995), is to follow the movement of actors, objects, cultural scripts and artefacts. The ethnographer moves through a spatially diverse and dispersed field via sojourns in two or more places. This involves constructing the empirical field by indicating various geographic localities. To be more precise, it enables the organization of research designs, methods of data collection and data interpretation. Scholars make increasing use of multi-sited ethnography not only because it justifies simultaneous research in different geographic localities and social sites, but also because it provides insights into the complexity of transnational phenomena (Falzon 2009). Instead of looking at social life in a single container, multi-sited ethnography is interested in the extension of social and symbolic ties across various sites. While earlier theorists situated their case studies within a world system and compared sites within that framework, those employing multi-sited ethnography start from the assumption that the world system is embedded in the sites analysed. The particular suitability of multi-sited ethnography for migration research results from understanding the sites of an empirical field as both territorial *and* social or cultural entities by following peoples and artefacts.

The growing popularity of multi-sited ethnography can also be explained by pragmatic reasons. There has been a tendency towards shorter stays in the field, shorter stays in various sites. Also, in order to gain depth, repeated short-term stints in the same sites have become more frequent. Furthermore, multi-sited ethnography does not rely on a strong theoretical orientation to guide empirical research. Rather, the ethnographer develops a framework out of the field research.

An example of this methodological approach is shown in Cindy Horst's study of refugees from Somalia in camps in north-east Kenya. She explicitly introduces a transnational perspective to the study in pursuing an approach she calls 'dialogical knowledge creation' (2006: 27). According to Horst, research methods have to 'involve dialogue between refugees, agencies and academics, leading to an exchange and discussion of ideas, concepts

148

and theories' (ibid.: 25) and to trace the multi-sited character of refugee life. Horst's procedure involved participatory approaches that actively engaged Somali refugees, policy-makers and practitioners in both data collection and analysis. For example, she discussed her research questions and methods with refugees and shared interview reports, fieldwork reports and, later, articles and preliminary chapters. The dialogue continued after Horst left the camps and involved research in various countries. She contacted refugees living in Western countries, published articles on diaspora websites, and solicited feedback and suggestions. She also sent her findings to the UN and received responses from policy-makers, UN and NGO staff, and researchers. Horst thus connected a participatory approach with multi-sited fieldwork. The research had a notable transnational dimension in another respect. The links that Somalis maintain with relatives outside the camps are essential for their daily survival. These links, which Horst traces through interviews, document analysis and participant observation, reach relatives throughout the larger cross-border diaspora. The transnational channels of the diaspora included the *taar* (radio communication transmitters), the telephone, the sending of messages and goods via those travelling to places where relatives lived, and *xawilaad*, an informal value-transfer system which enables both communication and the sending of remittances. In sum, Horst adapts her research methods to analyse Somali refugees in the camps as a transnational community which is linked across state borders to other Somalis elsewhere and to a host of international organizations and institutions. In this context she speaks of a 'diaspora mentality' (ibid.: 34) which brought advantages for Somalis in Dadaab and which fosters an extensive transnational network of relatives.

Mobile ethnography is a method of more recent vintage in which the correspondence between the mobility of people and the methods of researchers is placed at the fore. It addresses directly the spatial movement of people in transnational social spaces through direct observation of the associated social practices, such as sending remittances or organizing in associations. This approach begins with mobilities and patterns of geographical movements, not with groups, potentially averting the essentialism identified above by avoiding an exclusive focus on migrants solely as ethnic or national groups. Mobile ethnography has been inspired by multi-sited ethnography and offers insights 'into a multitude of mobile, material, embodied practices of making distinctions, relations and places' (Büscher et al. 2010: 105). Even more than multi-sited research, it focuses on the social practices of spatial mobility. This strategy recommends collecting data by 'observing people's mobility', 'walking with', 'stalking' or 'lurking' around others and enables researchers to define geographic and virtual mobility as an empirical field.

The specific value of multi-sited ethnography as one of the most widespread methods for transnational research emerges in comparison with another approach which also seeks to find out how sites connect to one another – namely, global ethnography, which builds on the extended case method developed in anthropology and adapted by sociological researchers (Burawoy et al. 2000). There are three major differences between these two approaches. First, multi-sited ethnography focuses on sites in various countries, whereas the main concern of global ethnography is the different scales of analysis – in other words, global ethnography is concerned with how the local and the global interact. For example, one of its central concerns is how global discourses on human rights are adopted and adapted by local social movements. Second, the two approaches differ in their understanding of context. In multi-sited ethnography, the context evolves out of the researcher discovering and delineating her own field. In global ethnography, the overall context is largely predefined by concepts that are important to existing theories. For example, in world system theories this would be capitalism, which structures the choices of the agents involved. To take another example, citizenship theories would emphasize mechanisms of democratization enabling citizens to act as full members of a polity or even multiple polities (see also chapter 6). Third, the role of theory in the construction of the research design differs in a significant way: theoretical constructs are held in abeyance in multi-sited ethnography but play a crucial role in global ethnography. In other words, there is a much stronger ambition in global ethnography to contribute to the modification of existing theories.

Multi-sited matched samples

One of the most systematic extensions of multi-sited research is the method of matched sampling, the so-called simultaneous matched sampling method (Mazzucato 2008). This is based on one of the main ideas of the transnational approach, namely the possibility of simultaneity – the overlapping or plurality of ties reaching into more than one site, in this case multiple sites in more than one country. The method thus considers the simultaneity of the transnational practices of individuals and groups taking place in multiple localities. The focus is on transactions involving communication and the movement of goods and on the networks of those who have migrated and those who have remained behind. Mazzucato and her colleagues used (non-representative) snowball sampling among migrants from Ghana in Amsterdam and traced their transactions back to two sites in the emigration state, in the capital Accra and in rural villages and towns in a region in the north of the country, around Kumasi. Working with over 100 migrants in Amsterdam, the researchers came up with twenty-nine networks. They recorded all transactions on a monthly basis conducted in eight domains (housing, business, funerals, church, health care, education, communication and community development projects) for a year in 2003–4. Different researchers thus worked in sites in both the Netherlands and Ghana and communicated quasi-simultaneously about the linkages between their respective parties. In this way this method aimed to overcome one of the limitations of multi-sited research – the fact that individual researchers usually cannot capture the simultaneity of transactions. Of critical importance is the fact that this method allows for tracing two-way flows between transnational sites – for example, 'reverse remittances' from Ghana to the Netherlands used for the legalization of undocumented migrants, financial remittances from Amsterdam to Kumasi or Accra, or the finding of a marriage partner. A specific focus was on the impact of migrant

*this conte show impacts of migrants in
other locations back in their country or
vice versa*

linkages on their home country's institutions via rules, values and norms that shape the economies of both their place of residence and their home communities. For example, transnational practices around funerals led to institutional change; the researchers found that funerals were one of the main reasons why migrants remain engaged with their home communities and continued to send remittances there. Investing in funerals both demonstrated the help they were giving and re-established and legitimized their position within the family and the home community despite the geographical distance. Migrants were the main financers of funerals (often having to borrow money from their network members based in the Netherlands). In turn, these practices yielded positive economic effects in the home community. For example, villagers and bars hosted and fed funeral guests (Mazzucato 2006).

Virtual networks

To uncover organizational structures and orientations of migrants' political online activities, Kissau and Hunger (2010) chose the Internet as a research site. The challenges for research are formidable because the Internet is a dynamic construct whose content, pages and user profiles may change daily. Nonetheless, as the Internet enables communication between members of a group dispersed across national state borders, a website analysis can yield valuable insights into communication networks. The researchers made a structured website search with the help of search engines and the snowballing method and came up with about 800 websites for the three groups in Germany under analysis – Turks, Kurds and Russians. In order to capture this moving target, they drew on a variety of research methods, out of which three proved to be most important. First, they conducted an analysis of the structure of the websites, using hyperlink analysis to uncover virtual networks. Second, they surveyed the sites' users and operators to detect individual interests and practices beyond the collective representations presented. Third, they selected about thirty websites for a detailed content analysis of pages created and used by migrants for political activities. Here the researchers looked at characteristics such as the thematic orientation, self-description and group boundaries. This virtual network methodology helped them to classify the type of Internet community, to acquire insights into the internal interaction among migrants within the respective online communities, and to look at strategies of communication between these groups and their political environment. The researchers' methodological caveat needs to be taken seriously: they add that online analysis does not replace fieldwork. After all, online and offline worlds interact and are not independent of one another.

Surveying transnationality

So far, we have reviewed mainly qualitative methods. These methods serve to identify the phenomenon of cross-border ties and practices in transnational social spaces. They are also instrumental in advancing our understanding of the mechanisms relevant in (re)producing practices and spaces. In order to establish the prevalence and extent of transnational ties, practices and spaces and to identify the major factors associated with their emergence, we turn to quantitative methods.

Studies based on qualitative methods are often limited in that they examine transnationality among migrants who entertain cross-border ties without including a reference group. This drawback echoes a more general criticism of studies on transnationalism: 'They study cases of the phenomenon itself so it is difficult to say anything about the extent of the phenomenon and whether it is increasing' (Portes 2001: 182–3). There is usually no comparison group in such studies of people who did not migrate or those who returned home from the country of immigration. This is a result of what Portes called 'sampling on the dependent variable' – that is, migrants with transnational ties are not compared with suitable comparison groups, namely those without cross-border links. Therefore, while qualitative studies were able to document the existence of transnational phenomena, we have little knowledge about their numerical prevalence. Also – and this is another crucial aspect not addressed by most existing studies – there is little evidence regarding the temporal dimension, either in historical perspective or across individual and family life courses (see chapters 3 and 5).

One of the most extensive surveys of transnational practices among migrants has been the Comparative Immigrant Entrepreneurship Project (CIEP) (Portes 2003; see chapters 2 and 5). Through quantitative fieldwork, supplemented by qualitative methods, this project focuses primarily on establishing the extent of transnational practices. The fieldwork was conducted between 1996 and 1998 among Colombian, Dominican and Salvadoran immigrant groups in the US, who represented, jointly, over one-fifth of Latin American immigrants at the time. The contexts of exit and reception of these groups were quite distinct. CIEP proceeded in two phases. Phase 1 comprised interviews with 353 key informants in six areas of immigrant concentration in the United States, two for each selected group, and in six foreign cities, including the capitals of each selected country of origin. Phase 2 consisted of a survey of the three immigrant groups in their principal areas of concentration in the United States, and proceeded in two stages. Stage 1 took a multi-level random sample based on city blocks as the primary units, and a systematic random sample of household heads from the selected nationalities in each block. Stage 2 employed a referral sample, based on data gathered from informants in the first phase and conducted through multiple snowball chains, aimed at identifying immigrants involved in entrepreneurial activities in general and transnational activities in particular. Note that the snowball procedure ensured a sufficient number of transnational entrepreneurs for quantitative analysis but (deliberately) biased the sample in their direction.

With this design, Portes and his collaborators could gauge quantitatively the spread and extent of transnational activities in the economic, political and socio-cultural spheres. The share of transnationals did not exceed one-fifth within each group across the three realms of activities. Nonetheless, transnational practices were quite substantive among certain subcategories – for example, the self-employed and the politically active. Thus, though it turned out that transnationally active migrants – defined as those who entertained dense and continuous ties across borders – were in a minority, the phenomenon as such could be established with great vigour and certainty. This kind of survey acts as a corrective to ethnographic studies that sometimes make it appear as though, for example, transnational entrepreneurship had become the main form of economic adaptation among contemporary immigrants. CIEP is an example of a cross-sectional study with data from specific points in time. Yet only longitudinal studies allow for results which establish a historical trajectory of the phenomena observed.

A combination of large-scale surveys and in-depth anthropological work, the ethno-survey methodology used by the Mexican Migration Project (MMP) traces migration patterns across time between Mexico and the US (Massey 1987). It is of crucial importance for transnational methodology, although the original idea was not to match people in countries of emigration with those in countries of immigration. While the MMP was not designed to focus on transnationality, its elements are helpful for the further development of transnational methodology. Douglas Massey, Jorge Durand and their colleagues developed the ethno-survey as an alternative methodology to the customary immigration surveys, which have 'serious inadequacies with respect to measuring undocumented migration' (Durand and Massey 2006: 321). The ethno-survey is a multi-method data-gathering technique that applies ethnographic and survey methods simultaneously within a single study. Two qualitative components, ethnographic case studies in the selected communities and in-depth interviews, are put together with a quantitative survey which is based on a combination of random and non-random sampling procedures. The combination of quantitative and qualitative methods corresponds to what is now called a mixed-methods design and proceeds as follows. First, the researchers select a site and start with conventional ethnographic fieldwork, including participant observation, unstructured in-depth interviewing and archival work. Data from this initial phase are then available for designing the survey instrument. The survey is administered to a probability sample of respondents selected according to a carefully designed plan (ibid.: chapter 13). Qualitative fieldwork continues during the survey or resumes after its completion. Ideally, the flow of analysis is organized so as to make preliminary quantitative data from the survey available to ethnographic investigators before they leave the field, allowing patterns emerging from quantitative analysis to shape qualitative fieldwork, just as insights from early ethnographies guide later statistical studies.

Originally the researchers surveyed four communities in Mexico. The data gathered include complete histories of migration, work and border crossings for all household heads and spouses; basic information on the first and most recent US trips of all household members with migratory experience; and detailed information about experiences on the most recent international trip made by the household head. So far, the MMP has surveyed eighty-one binational communities in Mexico and the US and yielded data on nearly 18,000 current and former US migrants. Although the data are of 'limited generalizability' and are not representative of Mexico or Mexican immigrants in general, they are useful for portraying and analysing aggregate trends.

The two surveys discussed, and studies in progress such as the German–Turkish Panel Study (Faist et al. 2011), constitute significant steps forward on at least three fronts. First, we normally have only national data for social ties and practices that cross nation-state boundaries. There is a deeper epistemological problem already alluded to: the evolution of survey research has been closely linked to the development of national states and thus also their needs. Second, many of the existing studies tend to presume the sedentary nature of the researched population. Therefore, most cross-country (internationally) comparative samples, such as the European Labour Force Surveys (ELFS), are known to under-sample along certain categories of activities. For example, ELFS does not cover mobile categories of persons, such as seasonal migrants or undocumented workers (for instance, in domestic and care services) because those not covered in the destination country will not necessarily be covered in the country of origin. Third, both CIEP and the ethno-survey include elements of qualitative research even though their logic is quantitative. They thus implement mixed-method designs. Qualitative methods are important because they are indispensable for determining reasons for errors in coverage and the effects of different sampling strategies. Moreover, in both surveys, interviews were not simply carried out with the help of standardized questionnaires but involved intensive conversations between interviewers and respondents to collect information perhaps missed by the standard questionnaire (e.g. patterns of mobility of household members). In essence, we need ways to capture the continuous multi-directional mobility of migrants between states and regions and approaches that contextualize migration within a pluri-local spatial framework.

Capturing simultaneity

The methodology of cross-border analysis needs to be distinguishable from comparative research that focuses on entities such as nation-states as exclusive and bounded units of analysis. One of the most promising solutions is multi-sited ethnography – that is, carrying out research in the sites of agents' practices in various countries. Multi-sited research in its various expressions is built on the idea of letting go of homogenizing notions of society and nation, culture and ethnicity. As we have seen, the challenges of capturing simultaneity through other multi-sited research methods are tremendous but manageable. The preceding discussion has presented additional methods appropriate to transnationally informed methodology, such as online analysis or a mixed-method application of representative survey research. It stands to reason that more work is needed systematically to develop various forms of multi-sited research. What all methods have in common, however, is an agency- and process-oriented view of cross-border social phenomena.

The various methods based on multi-sited research as well as the extended case method and mixed methods serve many more objectives than simply unearthing patterns of mobility. Such methods, for example, are also intended to reflect and dissect the processes of borders and boundary creations that produce immobility and find their expression in, for example, walls, camps or detention centres. Equally important, these methods focus our attention on the transnational social spaces which are usually populated by both mobile and relatively immobile agents.

Future work on transnational methodology could also profit by distinguishing the transnational perspective from other approaches, such as the cosmopolitan one. In general, the transnational approach emphasizes a constructivist view of social space. The focus is on how transnational practices constitute and reproduce transnational social spaces – in other words, transnational circuits and transnational communities (chapter 3). By contrast, the cosmopolitan approach (Beck and Sznaider 2006) presupposes *a priori* the existence of a global societal space (and thus a global horizon of observation by agents and researchers), described as a 'global cosmopolitan condition', which is organized primarily in national states and is constantly criss-crossed by transnational networks. Also, the cosmopolitan approach already conceives of a global outlook as a positive phenomenon and does not sufficiently distinguish between empirical trends and normative desirability. Nonetheless, despite this crucial difference, there are also important similarities. The methodological consequence of both the transnational and the cosmopolitan approach is a distinction between multi-level modes of observation – transnational, global, national, local – and actors' strategies that are calibrated along multiple scales.

8

Transnationalizing Civil Society

Civil society is central for understanding social processes, as it complements other principles of social order, mainly the family, the state and the market. And it is also central for cross-border transactions which concatenate into various forms of transnational social spaces. Since we deem it crucial to analyse cross-border practices and their concatenation in transnational structures, it is equally important systematically to evaluate the significance of transnationality and transnational social spaces for social order more generally. Civil society is especially useful because it is a principle of social order which is distinct but cross-cuts the other three principles just mentioned (see figure 8.1). On a concrete level, civil society often refers to the practices of non-state, non-market and non-family agents in the public sphere, where individuals and groups freely get together to identify and discuss issues of general interest, and thus shape political life. The importance of potential agents in civil society has been addressed at various places in this book, such as the relevance of hometown associations as agents of economic development (chapter 4), their role in migrant integration processes (chapter 5) and their participation in the politics of emigration and immigration states (chapter 6).

We now discuss civil society as a principle of social order more systematically by pursuing the question as to the relevance of cross-border ties and practices in transnational social spaces for the changing dynamics of civil society. This will help us to

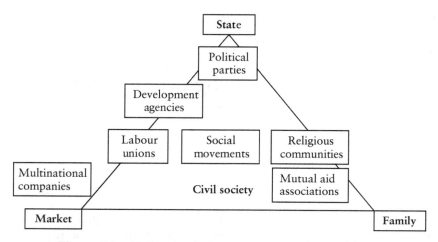

Figure 8.1 Civil society in between state, market, and family

understand some of the implications of transnational practices in contention around public issues, such as development, human rights, democratization or social justice. Overall, civil society – and this is the main proposition of this chapter – can fruitfully be thought of as transnationalizing civil society. This thesis refers back to the idea that, by tracing cross-border practices, we can begin to understand the consequences of social formations for public affairs.

In the following, we first look at the relationship between civil society and transnational social spaces and then recapitulate issues from the previous chapters that deal with or have relevance for civil society. Third, we analyse in a systematic way the interpenetration by civil society of each of the other principles of social order – market, state and family. Fourth, we address the questions of how transnational social spaces may contribute to transnationalizing civil society and of what the possibilities are for migrants to shape civil society. Fifth, we discuss how a transnational perspective on civil society informs social science thinking on mobilities and inequalities more generally.

Civil society and transnational social spaces

There is no generally accepted definition of civil society. It is an ambiguous and often incoherently used concept. Above all it is a normative concept that needs to be handled with care to avoid simply advancing the noble myth about global or transnational civil society as an engine for reforming the capitalist world system, improving upon the anarchical system of states and abolishing patriarchy in families. Instead it is necessary to begin by noting the often contradictory processes associated with this concept.

Civil society is not the monopoly of authority (the state), the price-finding/determining mechanism of supply and demand (the market) or a small-scale system of solidarity and reciprocity (the family). Most contemporary definitions of civil society are very general – for example, the idea that it is 'the arena, outside of the family, the state, and the market where people associate to advance common interests' (Civicus, n.d.). In a nutshell, civil society refers to various participatory institutions in social life, such as associations and organizations that are engaged in lobbying to change state policy, providing social protection against life risks such as unemployment and illness, or contributing to educational institutions. Very often, civil society is referred to when speaking of the potential for social change – for example, in accounts which refer to it as the arena of free collective action around shared interests, purposes and values. The agents most commonly referred to in civil society are registered charities, trusts, trade unions, citizens' protest groups, not-for-profit non-governmental organizations, community groups, women's organizations, faith-based organizations, professional associations, self-help groups, social movements, business associations, small and large corporate firms, state-independent media and advocacy groups. Hopes will often become attached to civil society as the seedbed and diffusion mechanism of democratization, human rights and gender equity.

Going against the perspective of this normatively loaded understanding of civil society, various voices have questioned, for example, how democratic civil society actually is. Some have noted that a number of civil society actors, such as globally operating human rights or environmental organizations, have now acquired a remarkable amount of political power without having been directly elected or appointed. Such organizations are not accountable to those for whom they claim to speak and thus lack formal legitimation. Critics have further argued that civil society is biased towards the Global North, whose civil society organizations dominate this sphere. For still others, civil society is a neo-colonial project driven by global elites in their own interests (Chatterjee 2004). And civil society agents may act not as the champions of non-violence, but quite the opposite. In the previous analysis we have encountered some diaspora groups that contribute to and shape nationalist movements for state-formation (chapter 6). In other words, diasporas are ambiguous in that they may be the conduit of normatively desirable social remittances or the contributors to bloody and protracted violence. We must therefore move beyond a conception of civil society which emphasizes only cooperation, empathy and public trust; the Janus face of civil society is also of interest. By opening up our understanding of civil society as a realm that comprises a broad range of outcomes – from normatively desirable to detrimental – we can more rigorously pursue the leading questions about the relevance of transnationality.

In the literature on transnationalization there has been a trend towards viewing migrant transnational practices as expressions of an essentially grassroots phenomenon (Portes 1996). In this vein, transnational practices are classified mainly as arising from below, in contrast to transnational relations generated from above through powerful actors such as multinational companies. In such a view, transnational practices would be part and parcel of a cross-border civil society. Yet the equation of 'transnationalism from below' with the empowerment of groups hitherto excluded from the benefits of cross-border transactions has been aptly criticized, since there are also instances of exploitation and oppression in small-scale cross-border groups; a case in point is exclusion based on patriarchy in certain family decision-making processes along gendered lines (Mahler 1998). Nonetheless, exclusion sometimes does not go unchallenged, and struggles are carried into the public sphere. Thus, civil society is above all 'an arena of struggle, a fragmented and contested area' (Keck and Sikkink 1998: 33). In civil society, the heterogeneities of class, race, gender and other markers, which are strongly associated with inequalities and injustices, are challenged by activists and leaders of social movements, ranging from human rights advocates to those who strive from a distance to establish a new national state. Those inequalities may be evolving to contribute either to horizontal solidarity or, in the negative case, to a strengthening of the old binaries of man/woman, black/white, or assimilated/non-assimilated – and the establishment of new binaries as between ordinary labour migrants and highly skilled professionals, or the resurgence of old ones such as Islam/Christianity. Thus a transnational perspective does not imply an overly sanguine conception of civil society as a realm characterized by trust, empathy, human rights, non-violence and struggles against social inequalities: there are also civil society agents who engage, for example, in the exploitation of fellow migrants (Tilly 2005: chapter 10). Such considerations raise doubts about civil society as a sort of 'repair shop' (Alexander 2006) for the ills of national societies and the problems of governance beyond nation-states.

In essence, civil society is used here as a heuristic device to inquire into how social entities such as national states or cities experience ever-increasing pluralization – also across borders. Migration is one of the ways through which social formations such as nation-states have become more heterogeneous regarding the range of worldviews and lifestyles, the number of languages spoken, the national backgrounds of people living in them, and the legal status of residents. Elements of cross-border civil society formations have also emerged through the social activities of migrants, seasonal workers, expatriates, posted workers, *flâneurs*, the regulatory activities of states and the cross-border expansion of markets. Yet the transnational social spaces throughout the book are not synonymous with transnationalizing civil society. They are rather potential elements of civil society.

We need further to specify what we mean by a transnational perspective on civil society. There are two lines of inquiry which we follow in this chapter. The first concerns the genesis of elementary forms of transnational civil society *sui generis*. This is also the main line of inquiry followed in the existing literature on transnational or global civil society. This approach is evolutionary in the broad sense and can be traced along with the successive geographical expansion of civil society from city-states to nation-states to – ultimately – the world – a move towards 'global civil society' (Keane 2003). The second line complements the first with a focus on transnational practices and therefore transnationalization of existing societies. It concerns the cross-border practices of associations and organizations. In this view there are no dichotomies, such as the inner and outer, internal and external boundary, as foundational for an understanding of civil society, nor is there the idea that civil society has gradually evolved from city-state to nation-state to the world. Indeed, to some degree, it can now be thought of only as transnationalized civil society, on all levels (chapter 7) – local, national, supranational, global. Here we focus on this second meaning of civil society. We therefore do not propose to speak of it as an ideal-typical construct of a fully fledged transnational civil society in singular or plural incarnations. Yet diasporas and communities of exiles provide a picture of the elements of an incipient transnational civil society nourished by social movements engaged in such issues as environmental protection of the Amazon, greater autonomy for Indians in Mexico, or the human rights of refugees.

The relevance of development, social integration and citizenship for civil society

In dealing with substantive questions of development, integration, membership and politics, the discussions in the previous chapters has given us some idea of how transnationality is constitutive for a broad understanding of civil society.

In chapter 4 we examined one of the allegedly positive functions of migrant groups and organizations – namely, assistance in developing the regions of origin. For some years now international organizations, development organizations – both those based in certain states, such as Oxfam (the UK) and Misereor (Germany), and those that are international, such as the United Nations Development Programme (UNDP) and the World Bank – and some national states have touted migrants as ideal agents for supporting economic and political development of their (former) home countries. The debate is critically important, because development thinking, policy and practice has since the 1970s discarded the notion of the 'developmental state' and placed more hopes on market mechanisms and civil society agents as central to development. These conceptual and policy changes have also entailed shifting priorities in addressing issues of poverty, inequality, agricultural reform or industrialization. There has thus been a wholesale shift away from the national development state to local statehood, international organizations and (international) non-governmental organizations (NGOs), and from state-led markets to greater involvement by core civil society agents, ranging from development NGOs to migrant associations. We have a potential expansion in the numbers and types of agents that are now considered pivotal to civil society as 'grassroots' agents of development. It becomes appropriate to ask whether migrant associations involved in development issues are part of civil society, or part of the state because of co-optation by national and local governments. For example, in the context of France and Mali, quite a few migrant associations fulfil relevant functions for infrastructure development. Such associations are sometimes rather close to national and local power-holders in these countries and not easily distinguishable as independent entities.

As reported in chapter 5, much of the research dealing with immigrant integration issues has assumed, perhaps not surprisingly, that migrant associations serve primarily to ease the adaptation process in countries of immigration. While this is a fruitful assumption, it has often ignored the multifocal character of migrant associations beyond borders. There is no theory or conceptualization of the integration of groups and organizations akin to the theories of integration, such as assimilation and ethnic pluralism. Nonetheless, we found that, just as is the case at the personal level, at the associational level adaptation and transnationalization are not zero-sum orientations. While, on the one hand, there are migrant associations totally devoted to issues of adaptation in the immigration state and, on the other, those who focus on the country of emigration, there are also associations engaged in both, to varying degrees and shifting over time. And those migrants active in cross-border organizations are often firmly rooted in one site – a prerequisite for transnational activism that has also been observed in the study of social movements (Tarrow 2005).

A fruitful area of inquiry in the relationship between civil society and the foundations of statehood is citizenship, as suggested in chapter 6. Citizenship is not only about the rights and duties of citizens guaranteed by the state, but also about the principle of democracy and the affiliation to a collective, built on trust and reciprocity. At the centre of our concern with civil society is the question as to the importance of migrant associations for a democratic public sphere. Taking the example of Muslim organizations with cross-border contacts in Western Europe, there is a lively debate about their 'fit' – which refers to a longstanding issue of immigration going back to charges of disloyalty to the Catholic Church in the first part of the nineteenth century in the United States, described so well in Tocqueville's *Democracy in America* ([1835] 1988). These days loyalty is often discursively connected to a democratic outlook and liberal values, leaving those organizations not structured internally along democratic principles especially prone to attack. This aspect harks back to an old question of whether organizations need to be internally democratic in order to be counted as beneficial to civil society. Other issues pertain to the effectiveness of migrant organizations. For example, to what extent are these driving changes in citizenship rules in countries of emigration and immigration? However, the political role of migrant associations may not reside at the national level, since they are more often active at the local level (Moya 2005), and thus across national state borders in a translocal way. An example of a translocal association is the hometown association. In this way migrant associations may indeed contribute to civic-mindedness and thus to civil society at the local level across borders.

This brief review of some of the findings and questions raised about civil society in the previous chapters makes abundantly clear that the boundaries of civil society are fuzzy, as evidenced by the seemingly contradictory notion that even belligerent diasporas are sometimes considered part of it. We have seen as well that civil society should be conceptualized as including on the one hand free public action, based on common interests and addressing inequalities, and on the other hand those practices that generate inequalities. For all these reasons, it can be useful not to consider the four principles of social order as distinct but to look at them as related, perhaps even mutually constituting concepts (see figure 8.1 above). If we stick to this triangular conceptualization, civil society can be visualized as 'in between' the three other principles, resulting in the following main strands of relationships: civil society and the market, civil society and the state, and civil society and the family.

Historically, the distinctions between the four principles of social order have gradually evolved over the last centuries. The fourfold distinction dates back to, among others, the German philosopher G. F. W. Hegel and the political analyst Alexis de Tocqueville. First, Hegel ([1882] 1991) conceptualized civil society as a form of market society and as a realm separate from what he called political society or the state, standing for the satisfaction of individual interests and private property. He held that civil society had emerged at a particular period of capitalism and served the latter's interests: individual rights and private property. In capitalism, individuals leave families to enter the realm of economic competition. Second, for Hegel, in constituting the realm of capitalist interests, civil society may be prone to conflicts and inequalities. He claimed that only the political state has the capacity and authority to correct the faults of civil society – an idea completely opposed to present-day conceptions of civil society as a sort of repair shop for society and the state overall. Alexis de Tocqueville, after comparing despotic France and democratic America, contested Hegel, promoting the system of civilian and

political associations as a counterbalance to both liberal indi-
vidualism and the centralization of the state (Tocqueville [1835]
1988). Nonetheless, both scholars thought it quite important that
civil society be analysed in conjunction with state, family and
markets. It was Karl Marx who was the first to conceptualize civil
society and, by implication, the market as borderless principles,
whereas states have taken the historical form of national states
(Marx and Engels [1845] 2011). This means that Marx thought
of both market and civil society as principles which are liberated
from the national state form, an idea that proves relevant for the
analysis of transnational phenomena.

Civil society and the state

Antonio Gramsci, taking up this debate on the role of the state
for civil society, and vice versa, did not consider civil society as
coterminous with the socio-economic base of the state. Rather,
he underlined its crucial role as the contributor of the cultural
and ideological resources required for the survival of capitalism
but also as a site which offered opportunities for the emergence
of what he called 'counter-hegemony'. Rather than posing it as
a problem, as in earlier Marxist conceptions, Gramsci viewed
civil society as the site for counter-hegemonic problem-solving
(Gramsci 1971). For Gramsci, the link between civil society
and the state is bureaucracy and the legal system. In support of
Gramsci's thought, the New Left in the 1960s and 1970s assigned
civil society a key role in defending people against the state and the
market and in asserting the democratic will to influence the state.
In contrast, thinkers in the 1980s have considered civil society as
a site for struggle to subvert communist and authoritarian regimes
and to move towards democracy.

For all the emphasis of social theory and political action on the
distinction between civil society and the state, there are certain
prerequisites which entail a mutually constitutive relationship.
First, some sort of state authority needs to guarantee a modicum
of human, civil, political and social rights for members. Second,

civil society agents and their associations need to have some autonomy from the state. And, third, there needs to be some social space for pluralistic political life. We will take up each of these prerequisites for civil society in turn. While they are necessary in order to speak of the normative project of civil society vis-à-vis the state, let us emphasize again that it is by no means certain that the final outcome will be democratization, equality for all members of civil society, and pluralistic political life.

A modicum of human, civil, political and social rights

Some human and civil rights have been codified in international conventions. There is, however, no overarching supranational structure effectively enforcing these rights throughout the world, no global government and no global civil society. Specific kinds of national states ensure these rights: liberal-democratic nation-states grant human, civil and social rights. At the international level, nation-states adhere to some degree to a regime of human rights as expressed in their consent to the Geneva Convention for Refugees (1951). At the nation-state level, basic civil and social rights are relatively independent of citizenship and are by now available to virtually all authorized migrants in liberal-democratic polities. And illegal immigrants are provided with emergency help and basic human rights even though accessing these usually results in deportation. Nonetheless, it is true that there are gradations in the extent of rights that aliens, denizens and citizens are able to claim.

To be effective, formal rights need to be translated into substantive rights. Secondary associations at the community or state level have a role in shaping state–citizen ties because they can help to transform formal rights into substantive realities. Transnational social spaces lack the institutional structure required for this translation. Contemporary cross-border processes associated with migration exemplify the tension between differently developed political regimes and the extent to which human, civil, political and social rights are realized in different parts of the world. Non-governmental organizations such as Amnesty International and refugee organizations that engage in human rights work reflect the striving for meaningful human and civil rights across borders. Migrant associations engaged in development projects in their emigration country communities illustrate the quest for substantive social citizenship.

Associational autonomy from the state

In order to speak meaningfully of civil society, we need to discern the level of autonomy of voluntary associations from other spheres such as states, markets and family or kin groups. The autonomy of such associations can be conceptualized by their degree of freedom – that is, the distance from the three endpoints of families, states and markets. In this view, churches and social movements are among the most independent actors in national civil societies. Yet autonomy does not always mean that associations active across borders are necessarily interested in advancing basic rights and liberal-democratic pluralism. Some migrant associations evolve out of existing cross-border structures such as the Catholic Church. In this case, migrant groups themselves do not provide the backbone of organizational linkages but make use of the institutions of the Church to maintain and reproduce transnational ties (Schmitter Heisler 1985). In other words, they take advantage of a wider transnational organizational structure. This has been possible in cases of religious affinities, such as migration from Latin America to the US or from Italy to Germany. In addition, Muslim organizations may rally immigrant associations under the heading of *umma*.

Migrant associations do not necessarily constitute elements of civil society but can do so if they enjoy a certain degree of autonomy from their respective states. The higher the orientation towards the country of emigration of transnationally active organizations, the more the government of that country is likely to step up efforts at control. If these organizations engage in anti-regime activities, governments frequently exert pressure on their counterparts in the country of immigration to curtail political activities of immigrants and refugees. In this way, the autonomy of transnationally active organizations is always threatened.

Pluralist-liberal democracy

A functioning civil society flourishes in a pluralistic democracy that allows its members publicly to express and pursue collective and individual interests. Political competition, partisanship and conflicts between the various groups are basic ingredients. Civil society denotes a pluralistic society in which the sometimes varying obligations of its members, groups and communities towards central institutions and laws are recognized. It would be presumptuous to speak of contemporary transnational structures in which these requirements are fulfilled.

Overall, the relationship of civil society to the state is inherently ambiguous. On the one hand, civil society often supports the state, as has been the case with much of the Catholic Church in Latin America. Political activities from abroad sometimes also contribute to maintaining local and national political power relations (chapter 6). On the other hand, agents in and of civil society may oppose the state, as social movements have done repeatedly. Human rights groups that challenge the power practices of states are a case in point. Of course, one must be cautious not to get caught up in a static picture. Sometimes, social movements, protest movements or opposing diasporas may be co-opted by state authorities.

Civil society and the market

Lately, civil society in the form of migrant-led activities has appeared on the agenda of international development organizations. We discussed diasporas in the North that engage in development projects in their home regions in the South in chapter 4. This is but one instance of the political and economic significance of civil society in interpreting social transformation. Famously, Karl Polanyi ([1944] 2001) analysed the market fundamentalism of the nineteenth century and the response to it by civil society and states until the early 1940s. In his view, the reaction to market fundamentalism was the rise of authoritarian movements, culminating in fascism and Stalinism and two world wars. The constitution of the liberal political order after the Second World War occurred under the premise of 'embedded liberalism' in the Western world and as the 'developmental state' in what used to be called the Third World. Since the late 1970s, the notions of the welfare state in the North and state-led development in the South have come under vigorous attack. This trend started as a neo-conservative cum neo-liberal restructuring of welfare states under Ronald Reagan and Margaret Thatcher and a departure from state-led development through international organizations such as the International Monetary Fund (IMF) and its structural adjustment programmes. In the aftermath of this decisive political-economic transformation, the Washington Consensus of the 1990s, which involved conditional loans from the World Bank and the IMF to debt-laden developing states, created pressures for states to shrink their public sectors. This in turn led to practical changes for civil society that had an influence on the theoretical debate. Initially the new conditionality led to an even greater emphasis on civil society as a panacea, or magic bullet, to replace the service provision and social care provided by the state. According to this view, the market principle of an allocation of resources by way of a pricing mechanism is thought to be superior to the authoritative allocation of resources by the state. Since the late 1990s and early 2000s the principle of the market has made its way into how international organizations have depicted migrants as economic entrepreneurs and not just as labour migrants or refugees. The new enthusiasm on the part of OECD states and international organizations such as the World Bank for the crucial role of migrant networks and associations as development agents reflects the fact that community and – often used interchangeably – civil society as a principle of development have come to replace or at least supplement principles of social order such as the market and the state.

Civil society and the family

Cross-border migration today has resulted in the increased prevalence of what have been called transnational families – families with members living in different national states. Research on these families has been spurred by the understanding of the gendered nature of mobility, in particular the 'feminization of migration' – that is, the fact that there has been an increasing proportion of women migrating independently and not only moving as spouses joining their husbands or remaining separated. Of special interest is that more and more transnational families remain spatially separated, whether as a result of newer types and patterns of migration or because of restrictive immigration laws (chapter 2). But at the same time we see that migrants can now stay in touch with loved ones more easily owing to cheaper travel conditions, the Internet and other forms of telecommunication previously unavailable. Still, we do not know how pervasive transnational families really are. Another crucial aspect is how transnationality – that is, the degree to which families and individuals are engaged in transactions across borders – may depend on and change over the life course. For example, transnationality may be high in the age range from twenty to forty, when the propensity for family formation, geographical mobility and labour market participation overlap. Therefore, the issues raised concerning transnational families – transnational fatherhood and motherhood, the roles of sons and daughters, and the involvement of families in transnational social movements – need to be seen against the backdrop of the life course in and of families.

In connecting transnational families to civil society, two points arise. First, issues such as transnational motherhood have surfaced as moral issues in the public sphere through mass media. Second, transnational families raise new questions about involvement of migrants in larger communities.

First, though there is scant knowledge about transnational families, there are vigorous public and policy debates, in emigration regions of Eastern Europe in particular, about the impact of transnational motherhood on families and children and on the role of civil society and the local state. Among the main agents involved in public debate are the mass media, which also form a key element of civil society. For example, popular news magazines in some Eastern European countries have described the children abandoned by migrants as 'Euro orphans', whose 'bad' mothers decided to go to the West in order to seek personal fulfilment through taking advantage of new economic opportunities without considering the negative impacts on their vulnerable children (Lutz and Palenga-Möllenbeck 2012). Such accounts focusing on the elderly and the children who are left to fend for themselves after the migration of women to Western Europe usually make no mention of altered conditions for work. Certainly, the picture is much more complex than the one depicted by the mass media. Ethnographic evidence from different parts of the world suggests that migrant women often leave children in the care of substitute mothers, their fathers or the extended family (Parreñas 2001b). However, we do not know, for example, how such care is dealt with in Romania, Ukraine and Poland. It is useful therefore to look in detail at the mechanisms underlying displacement and substitution of care. It is also necessary to understand the reorganization of care in immigration regions and the consequences for both these and emigration regions ('care drain') as part of a larger 'global care chain' – a concept inspired by the idea of commodity chains (Yeates 2009). While one should not minimize the potential feelings of loss that many of the children in transnational families must experience when separated from their main care giver, it is also important to be careful about applying notions of sedentary mothering or parenting to migration contexts. It may be useful to gain a better understanding of the practices of cross-border motherhood and the actual impact on children. An example of the policy debates can be found in the context of care work by Ukrainian women in Italy, who are faced with difficulties in finding even irregular work, but also in finding child care at home, and thus are engaged in long-distance parenting. Interestingly, in Ukraine, there are policy debates at the local level on how to take care of the elderly and how to cope with problems of discipline in schools (Piperno 2007).

Second, if we recall that domestic and private life are not insulated from their wider social sphere, and that families play a role in public life, it is likely that all relative and peer relations, not just relations between partners, parents and children, are reconfigured by transnational life courses. An obvious instance is migrant associations or religious congregations, whose membership often consists of families. Religious associations of African migrants in Germany, for example, fulfil manifold spiritual but also social support functions. In some cases, women are very active in providing support for community services behind the scenes (Sieveking 2011). Changing gender relations within families are mirrored in civil society activities in other ways. There are also instances where women have taken to the streets. The Mexican women farmworkers' organization Líderes Campesinas has marched in the streets of Californian cities to protest against domestic violence (see Hondagneu-Sotelo 2000).

The role and function of migrant transnational social spaces for civil society

Having reviewed the fluid boundaries between the social organizational principles of civil society vis-à-vis state, market and family, it is possible to take a closer look at how migrant transnational social spaces tie in with civil society. As an analytical perspective, a transnational approach focuses both on cross-border practices and on how 'old' institutional structures at the local and national level change in the context of transnationalization. In the realm of politics, a transnational approach has to account for both transborder nationalism and nation-transcending conceptions of political community without being committed to either. With respect to the economic realm, a transnational approach has to deal with both the opportunities of small-scale entrepreneurs across borders and the exploitation of close kin. As to the sociocultural realm, a transnational approach has to pay attention not only to how opportunities for transnational families to ensure income are enlarged but also to how and what types of oppressive relations are sustained.

A helpful starting point for understanding how migrants and their significant others are involved in shaping transnationalizing civil society is Jonathan Fox's notion of 'migrant civil society'. By this term he understands 'migrant-led membership organizations and public institutions' (Fox 2007). His migrant civil society lies at the interstices of places, organizations and people in countries of emigration and immigration. In our terminology it would be premature to speak of transnational or global civil society, let alone of civil society made up primarily of one category of agents such as migrants, as in the term 'migrant civil society'. This would be stretching the concept too far. Yet it is worth looking at the elements that contribute to civil society out of transnational social spaces and how the latter are shaped by civil society. Two prominent examples in which the web of cross-border ties is quite dense are those between the US and Mexico and between Turkey and Germany (Goldring and Krishnamurti 2007; Faist and Özveren 2004). We then need to establish which elements of such a cross-border space are relevant. The associational activities could either be migrant-led or have a strong element of migrant involvement. Crucial elements of transnationalizing civil societies arising out of cross-border social spaces are (1) migrant membership organizations, (2) migrant-led NGOs and (3) migrant-run communication media, coupled with (4) autonomous migrant-led public spaces and (5) a consciousness of the importance of cross-border transactions.

First, membership organizations are clubs and associations, such as hometown associations, which cater exclusively to the needs of migrants and non-migrants in the localities of origin. Second, NGOs may take the form of established non-profit associations, which serve not only their members but also other migrant group members, and which are led by migrants. Migrant membership associations and NGOs may rally around diverse heterogeneities. There may be ethno-national organizations (including indigenous entities), religious associations, multi-ethnic organizations and anti-discrimination movements – to name only a few. The two elements discussed so far could be either of migrant origin or with substantive migrant participation. Migrant-led associations establish themselves in order to realize a diverse range of activities. Migrants could also be involved in already existing associations. An example would be workers' organizations, in which migrants band together because they identify with other workers in the same labour context. A case in point is UNITE HERE!, which is the organization of the hotel, gaming, food service, manufacturing, textile, distribution, laundry and airport industries in the United States. During recent decades the importance of Mexican workers and their organizations for the American labour unions has increased, as they are present in exactly those regions and sectors where unions are dynamic and are recruiting new members (Haus 2002). Third, communication media refer to forms of representation, such as web pages, newspapers, magazines or radio programmes, in the receiving or sending region, or in both. The media may encompass local, binational newspapers, radio programmes and independent Internet discussion fora (see Madianou and Miller 2012). Fourth, the concept of autonomous migrant-led public spaces refers to migrants displaying their claims, as in rallies, large gatherings and demonstrations. A very visible case in point was 'The Great American Boycott' (Spanish: *El Gran Paro Estadounidense*) in 2006. Immigrants in the US without papers, hailing mostly from Latin America, engaged in a one-day boycott of schools and businesses. Such protests are intimately connected to cross-border transactions. For example, the Mexican government has issued identity cards to migrants without legal residence and work status. These cards are recognized in some US states as valid documents for legal transactions such as obtaining a driver's licence. The fifth element is the awareness of the significance of cross-border transactions. In transnationalizing civil society, the major point is not only that transactions cross the borders of nation-states through the activities of membership organizations, NGOs, practices in public spheres and mass media. Agents need to have an idea of the importance of forging links across borders, be they ties out of loyalty to their home village, former state or family, or the realization that certain issues, such as human rights, spill across borders. Consciousness of cross-border transactions and social practices, which often directly affect those who are active, go hand in hand. While these five elements do not necessarily constitute a transnational migrant civil society, they are part and parcel of civil society and show how migrants' cross-border practices shape civil society.

Migrants may use transnational ties and turn to supranational and international bodies to advance their interests and further their goals. First, there are migrant organizations which have been established in countries of immigration and engage in networking and promotion of public affairs in their places of origin. A noteworthy example is the Turkish Alevi organizations in Europe, which have sprung up in various European countries. While these started out predominantly as supporters of social democratic parties in the countries of immigration, they eventually evolved into associations defined by the Alevi religious belief system and expanded 'back' into Turkey (Bak Jørgensen 2008: chapter 8). Another example is provided by Mexican migrant organizations abroad which fund public works and social projects in their communities of origin without the aid of the government-sponsored programme 'Tres por Uno'. From the other side of the equation, there are membership organizations which have been established in countries of emigration and engage in transactions across borders. An example is the Islamic organization Milli Görüş, which originated in Turkey but has extended into such European countries as Germany and the Netherlands (Carkoğlu 2009). Second, the focus could be on countries of immigration while also engaging in countries of emigration. An example is the cooperation of California's migrant-based Oaxacan Federation with US-based labour unions in the 2003 Immigrant Worker Freedom Ride, patterned after the African-American civil rights movement Freedom Rides into the American South during the early 1960s. Activists from both labour unions and migrant organizations joined together to take their demands for legalization and rights at work to Washington, DC.

Are the agents just mentioned part of American as opposed to Mexican civil society, or part of German as opposed to Turkish civil society? The answer to this question brings us back to our original proposition. We have claimed that it is fruitful to speak of transnationalizing civil society rather than juxtaposing national civil society and transnational civil society. Civil society nowadays has to be comprehended by looking both at how old institutions in national states are changing and how new institutions are emerging beyond the nation-state. The answer is that they belong to transnationalizing civil society, which can be understood as being constituted by the cross-border practices analysed throughout this book.

These reflections also bear out our differentiation of the term transnational made in the introductory chapter. Transnationalization has proven to be a useful concept to describe the process of the cross-border expansion of social space. This term thus reaches beyond the field of migration studied in this book and can be applied to key and master concepts in the social sciences, in this case civil society. Transnational activities, a reflection of migrants' transnationality, are part of larger social structures called transnational social spaces. As we have seen, such transnational social spaces are not coterminous with civil society. Nonetheless, transnational social spaces need to be considered to gain a better understanding of how various sites across borders are interconnected by migrants and non-migrants alike, as well as their organizations and institutions. Cross-border practices in transnational social spaces may contribute to transnationalizing civil societies.

Migrants and their often relatively immobile significant others, as suggested in the individual chapters of the book, can be active participants in civil society. What is important to keep in mind is that agents active across borders are not uniform with respect to the intensity, extent or durability of their ties. We therefore need to consider the different degrees of transnationality, which allows us always to keep in mind that cross-border transactions never simply stand on their own but are connected back to places.

The significance of a transnational approach for the social sciences

As we suggested at the beginning of this book, in discussing the film *The Edge of Heaven*, it is not possible to make clear-cut attributions with respect to the social integration of immigrants and, by implication, of individuals connected to others around the world. Linear stories of mono-local activities and memberships are there, but they are not the only game in town. A transnational approach does not view cross-border activities and practices or membership in multiple states as a necessary consequence of globalizing modernity, as if the European and North American models of political, economic and cultural development are now spreading across the world in a linear fashion. Such a view would simply posit another container – this time at the world level rather than at the nation-state level. Instead of a view which sees a European-style process of functional differentiation across the world, a transnational lens holds that it is fruitful to look at how the various social formations and practices across the borders of national states and across the globe are interlinked through transactions. The main point is not abstract linkages, as in globalization theories, but to take into account transnational practices by analysing processes of transnationalization, the social structures of transnational spaces and transnationality as a heterogeneity and thus as a marker of agents. The world across borders is constituted by transnational practices, and this implies a research agenda tracing such practices.

The practices under consideration must also be those of researchers. Much more attention needs to be paid to reflect the power asymmetries both in and outside the world of research. In migration research, the overwhelming majority of studies see mobilities and inequalities from the perspective of the immigration state, bringing in the emigration side only when talking about issues such as migration and development. A transnational perspective seeks to rectify this exclusion. Much of the research is carried out, or is at least financed by institutions and researchers, in immigration countries. Therefore, positionality needs to be reflected, even if the research is concerned mainly – with an immigration perspective – as is also true for this book. The attention to power differentials also gives us important clues for thinking about truly worldwide questions such as inequalities. It is not only inequalities between regions of the world that are at the root of migration, and migration is not only a strategy to overcome poverty or improve one's life chances. But inequalities between people residing in different parts of the world do reflect unequal life chances across the globe.

Given the discussion on methodological nationalism and essentialism (chapter 7), one may ask whether the transnational approach could be extended to include not only cross-border transactions but all sorts of boundary-crossing phenomena. According to such an expansionist view, the transnational approach could now be assumed to be applicable to questions such as boundaries between groups, as in intergroup relations between migrants and dominant groups in both immigration and emigration states. It is certainly true that a transnational approach has similarities with boundary studies more generally, in that state borders connote a specific type of boundary. Yet, taken to extremes, the dissolution of the transnational approach into boundary studies would seriously overreach the meaning of the former. State borders are of particular relevance and have features which are not shared, for example, by boundaries between groups. State borders signify particular boundaries around membership with far-reaching consequences (citizenship) and also connote extensive claims to ways of equal liberty for political participation (democracy). Such principles are not institutionalized in other social formations to the same extent. To give up the borders of states, understood in a broad sense, as a defining feature of the transnational approach is to dissolve it into an amorphous mass of boundary studies which are held together by the metaphor of border. Much more important than an inflation of new terms is the specification of social mechanisms involved in transnational practices, and thus a contribution to theories of the middle range. For example, we need to understand how mechanisms such as stereotyping, reciprocity and solidarity, exclusion or inclusion, opportunity hoarding and hierarchization, structure cross-border life worlds and social spaces. Such modest theories tie the transnational approach into the wider agenda of the social sciences.

The various methods based on multi-sited research, as well as the extended case method and mixed methods, serve many more objectives than simply unearthing patterns of mobility. Such methods, for example, are also intended to reflect and dissect the processes of borders and boundary creations that produce immobility and find their expression in, for example, walls, camps or detention centres. Equally important, these methods focus our attention on the transnational social spaces which are usually populated by both mobile and relatively immobile agents.

Seen against this background, transnational social spaces and transnationalizing civil society are realities not only for migrants and their sometimes immobile significant others in family and friendship circles but also for non-migrants who trade with others, exchange mail or travel abroad. The research on transnational ties of categories other than migrants has just started, and there is a considerable challenge to integrate studies on migrants, expatriates, business people and social movement activists – to name a few of the more obvious categories. Last but not least, migration research can be integrated conceptually into other areas dealing with cross-border exchanges, such as social movements, advocacy networks or religious communities. Transnationality is not only a potential attribute of the heterogeneity of migrants and their families, it also affects other categories of individuals and groups in the context of transnational communalization (*Vergemeinschaftung*) and sociation (*Vergesellschaftung*) processes.

Notes

1 In late 2008, about 1,880,800 of a total of 15,150,400 refugees – that is, 12.4 per cent – stayed in least developed countries (UN 2009).
2 The literature on transnational ties on South–South migration is currently still too scant to serve as a basis for informed judgement. This is an important task for future research (see, for example, Leichtmann 2005).
3 The TRANS-NET project was carried out from 2008 to 2011 and involved partners from eight countries, which were grouped in four pairs: Estonia/Finland, India/the UK, Morocco/France and Turkey/Germany. Within these country contexts processes of transnationalization were analysed in the political, economic, socio-cultural and educational spheres (Pitkänen et al. 2012). The sample of the German survey included seventy-three qualitative interviews with Turkish citizens living in Germany, German citizens who were once Turkish citizens, and German citizens of whom at least 1 per cent were (formerly) Turkish citizens. As a result, the group of respondents consisted of categories such as former 'guest workers', asylum-seekers, marriage migrants, migrants based on family reunification, German-born children of Turkish migrants, foreign degree students and high-skilled labour migrants. The interviews were conducted in German and in the case studies quoted here have been translated into English. For findings of the TRANS-NET survey, see Gerdes et al. (2012), Gerdes and Reisenauer (2012) and Fauser and Reisenauer (2012).
4 For detailed information on transnational socio-cultural, economic and political practices among Colombian, Dominican and Salvadorian immigrants in the United States, see further publications from the CIEP (Portes 2001, 2003). For socio-cultural practices especially, see Itzigsohn and Saucedo (2002); for economic practices see Landolt (2001), Portes et al. (2002) and Guarnizo (2003); and, for political practices, see Guarnizo et al. (2003). For the CIEP, see also chapters 5 and 7.
5 For a current longitudinal study conducted from 2011 to 2015 at Bielefeld University, see the subproject 'Transnationality and Inequality: The Pilot

Project for the Panel Study' in the Collaborative Research Centre 'From Heterogeneities to Social Inequalities' (Faist et al. 2011; see also www.sfb882. uni-bielefeld.de/).

6 Much of the work using the NELM approach is on internal migration, with a focus on rural-to-urban movement, mainly in Africa, but it has been expanded to international migration premised upon the same theoretical concepts.

References

Abadan-Unat, N. (2011) *Turks in Europe: From Guest Worker to Transnational Citizen*. Oxford: Berghahn.

Al-Ali, N. (2002) Loss of status or new opportunities? Gender relations and transnational ties among Bosnian refugees, in D. Bryceson and U. Vuorela (eds), *The Transnational Family: New European Frontiers and Global Networks*. Oxford and New York: Berg, pp. 83–102.

Alba, R., and Nee, V. (2003) *Remaking the American Mainstream: Assimilation and Contemporary Immigration*. Cambridge, MA: Harvard University Press.

Albrow, M. (1996) *The Global Age: State and Society Beyond Modernity*. Cambridge: Polity.

Alexander, J. (2006) *The Civic Sphere*. New Haven, CT: Yale University Press.

Amelina, A. (2011) An intersectional approach to the complexity of social support within German–Ukrainian transnational space, in E. N.-L. Chow, M. T. Segal and L. Tan (eds), *Analyzing Gender, Intersectionality, and Multiple Inequalities: Global, Transnational and Local Contexts*. Bingley: Emerald, pp. 211–34.

Amelina, A., Nergiz, D., Faist, T., and Glick Schiller, N. (eds) (2012) *Beyond Methodological Nationalism: Research Methodologies for Cross-Border Studies*. London: Routledge.

Amelina, A., and Faist, T. (2012) De-naturalizing the national in research methodologies: key concepts of transnational studies in migration, *Ethnic and Racial Studies*, 35(10): 1707–24.

Aristotle (1962) *The Politics*. London: Penguin.

Bak Jørgensen, M. (2008) National and transnational identities: Turkish organising processes and identity construction in Denmark, Sweden and Germany, PhD dissertation, Aalborg University.

Bakewell, O. (2009) *South–South Migration and Human Development: Reflections on African Experiences*, UNDP Human Development Research Paper 2009/07, http://hdr.undp.org/en/reports/global/hdr2009/papers/HDRP_2009_07.pdf (accessed 10 July 2012).

References

Barth, F. (1969) *Ethnic Groups and Boundaries: The Social Organization of Cultural Difference*. Oslo: Universitetsforlaget.

Basch, L., Szanton Blanc, C., and Glick Schiller, N. (1994) *Nations Unbound: Transnational Projects, Postcolonial Predicaments and Deterritorialized Nation-States*. New York: Gordon & Breach/Routledge.

Bauböck, R. (1994) *Transnational Citizenship: Membership and Rights in International Migration*. Cheltenham: Edward Elgar.

Bauböck, R. (2003) Towards a political theory of migrant transnationalism, *International Migration Review*, 37(3): 700–23.

Beck, U. (1999) *What is Globalization?* Oxford: Blackwell.

Beck, U., and Sznaider, N. (2006) Unpacking cosmopolitanism for the social sciences: a research agenda, *British Journal of Sociology*, 57(1): 1–23.

Beck-Gernsheim, E. (2006) Transnationale Heiratsmuster und transnationale Heiratsstrategien: Ein Erklärungsansatz zur Partnerwahl von Migranten, *Soziale Welt*, 57(2): 111–29.

Bhagat, R. B. (2009) Internal migration in India: are the underclass more mobile?, paper presented at the IUSSP General Population Conference, Marrakech, Morocco, http://iussp2009.princeton.edu/download.aspx?submis sionId= 90927 (accessed 10 July 2012).

Bodnar, J. (1985) *The Transplanted: A History of Immigrants in Urban America*. Bloomington: Indiana University Press.

Bonifazi, C., Okólski, M., Schoorl, J., and Simon, P. (eds), (2008) *International Migration in Europe: New Trends and New Methods of Analysis*. Amsterdam: Amsterdam University Press.

Boyarin, J. (1994) *Remapping Memory: The Politics of Timespace*. Minneapolis: University of Minnesota Press.

Breton, R. (1964) Institutional completeness of ethnic communities and the personal relations of immigrants, *American Journal of Sociology*, 70(2): 193–205.

Brubaker, R. (2004) *Ethnicity without Groups*. Cambridge, MA: Harvard University Press.

Brubaker, R. (2005) The 'diaspora' diaspora, *Ethnic and Racial Studies*, 28(1): 1–19.

Bryceson, D. (2002) Europe's transnational families and migration: past and present, in D. Bryceson and U. Vuorela (eds), *The Transnational Family: New European Frontiers and Global Networks*. Oxford and New York: Berg, pp. 31–59.

Bryceson, D., and Vuorela, U. (2002) Transnational families in the twenty-first century, in D. Bryceson and U. Vuorela (eds), *The Transnational Family: New European Frontiers and Global Networks*. Oxford and New York: Berg, pp. 3–30.

Bühlmeier, D., Goetzke, J., and Di Salvo, A. (2011) Business on the move, business on the run, in T. Faist and N. Sieveking (eds), *Unravelling Migrants as*

References

Transnational Agents of Development: Social Spaces in between Ghana and Germany. Münster: Lit, pp. 29–68.

Burawoy, M., Blau, J. A., George, S., Gille, Z., Thayer, M., Gowan, T., Haney, L., Klawiter, M., Lopez, S. H., and Riain, S. (2000) *Global Ethnography: Forces, Connections and Imaginations in a Post-Modern World*. Berkeley: University of California Press.

Büscher, M., Urry, J., and Witchger, K. (2010) *Mobile Methods*. London: Routledge.

Çağlar, A. S. (2006) Hometown associations, the rescaling of state spatiality and migrant grassroots transnationalism, *Global Networks*, 6(1): 1–22.

Carkoğlu, A. (2009) *Religion and Politics in Turkey*. London: Routledge.

Castells, M. (1996) *The Information Age: Economy, Society and Culture*, Vol. 1: *The Rise of the Network Society*. Oxford: Blackwell.

Chan, K. B. (1997) A family affair: migration, dispersal, and the emergent identity of the Chinese cosmopolitan, *Diaspora. A Journal of Transnational Studies*, 6(2): 195–213.

Chatterjee, P. (2004) *The Politics of the Governed: Reflections on Popular Politics in Most of the World*. New York: Columbia University Press.

Christiansen, C. C. (2008) Hometown associations and solidarities in Kurdish transnational villages: the migration–development nexus in a European context, *European Journal of Development Research*, 20(1): 88–103.

Civicus (n.d.) *Civil Society Index: Summary of Conceptual Framework and Research Methodology*, www.civicus.org/new/media/CSI_Methodology_and_conceptual_framework.pdf (accessed 10 July 2012).

Coffey, A. (1996) The power of accounts: authority and authorship in ethnography, *International Journal of Qualitative Studies in Education*, 9(1): 61–74.

Cohen, R. (1997) *Global Diasporas: An Introduction*. London: UCL Press.

Collier P., and Hoeffler, A. (2000) *Greed and Grievance in Civil War*, Policy Research Working Paper. Washington, DC: World Bank.

Collier, P., and Hoeffler, A. (2002) *Greed and Grievance in Civil War*, Working Paper Series 2002-01. Oxford: Centre for the Study of African Economies.

Connell, R. A. (2009) *Southern Theory: The Global Dynamics of Knowledge in Social Science*. Cambridge: Polity.

Cordero-Guzmán, H. (2005) Community-based organisations and migration in New York City, *Journal of Ethnic and Migration Studies*, 31(5): 889–910.

Dannecker, P. (2005) Transnational migration and the transformation of gender relations: the case of Bangladeshi labour migrants, *Current Sociology*, 53(4): 655–74.

De Haas, H. (2008) *Migration and Development: A Theoretical Perspective*, Working Paper 9/2008. Oxford: International Migration Institute.

Della Porta, D., and Tarrow, S. (eds) (2005) *Transnational Protest and Global Activism*. Lanham, MD: Rowman & Littlefield.

References

Dişbudak, C. (2004) Transnational and local entrepreneurship, in T. Faist and E. Özveren (eds), *Transnational Social Spaces: Agents, Networks and Institutions*. Aldershot: Ashgate, pp. 143–62.

Donato, K. M., Hiskey, J., Durand, J., and Massey, D. S. (2010) Migration in the Americas: Mexico and Latin America in comparative context, *Annals of the American Academy of Political and Social Science*, 630(1): 6–17.

Dufoix, S. (2008) *Diasporas*. Berkeley: University of California Press.

Durand, J., and Massey, D. (eds), (2006) *Crossing the Border: Research from the Mexican Migration Project*. New York: Russell Sage Foundation.

Durand, J., Parrado, E. A., and Massey, D. S. (1996) Migradollars and development: a reconsideration of the Mexican case, *International Migration Review*, 30(2): 423–44.

Ezli, Ö. (ed.) (2010) Kultur als Ereignis: Fatih Akins Film 'Auf der anderen Seite' als transkulturelle Narration. Bielefeld: transcript.

Faist, T. (1997) Migration in contemporary Europe: European integration, economic liberalization, and protection, in J. Klausen and L. Tilly (eds), *European Integration in Social and Historical Perspective 1850 to the Present*. Boulder, CO: Rowman & Littlefield, pp. 223–48.

Faist, T. (1998) Transnational social spaces out of international migration: evolution, significance and future prospects, *Archives Européennes de Sociologie*, 39(2): 213–47.

Faist, T. (2000a) *The Volume and Dynamics of International Migration and Transnational Social Spaces*. Oxford: Oxford University Press.

Faist, T. (2000b) *Transstaatliche Räume: Politik, Wirtschaft und Kultur in und zwischen Deutschland und der Türkei*. Bielefeld: Transcript.

Faist, T. (2001) Social citizenship in the European Union: nested membership, *Journal of Common Market Studies*, 39(1): 39–60.

Faist, T. (2004a) The border-crossing expansion of social space: concepts, questions and topics, in T. Faist and E. Özveren (eds), *Transnational Social Spaces: Agents, Networks and Institutions*. Aldershot: Ashgate, pp. 1–36.

Faist, T. (2004b) Towards a political sociology of transnationalism, *European Journal of Sociology*, 45(3): 331–66.

Faist, T. (2007) *Dual Citizenship in Europe: From Nationhood to Societal Integration*. Aldershot: Ashgate.

Faist, T. (2008) Migrants as transnational development agents: an inquiry into the newest round of the migration–development nexus, *Population, Space and Place*, 14(1): 21–42.

Faist, T. (2009) Making and remaking the transnational: of boundaries, social spaces and social mechanisms, *Spectrum: Journal of Global Studies*, 1(2): 66–88.

Faist, T. (2010a) Towards transnational studies: world theories, transnationalization and changing institutions, *Journal of Ethnic and Migration Studies*, 36(10): 1665–87.

References

Faist, T. (2010b) Transnationalization and development: towards an alternative agenda, in N. G. Schiller and T. Faist (eds) *Migration, Development, and Transnationalization: A Critical Stance*. New York: Berghahn, pp. 63–99.

Faist, T. (2011) Academic knowledge, policy, and the public role of social scientists, in T. Faist, M. Fauser and P. Kivisto (eds),: *The Migration–Development Nexus: Transnational Perspectives*. Basingstoke: Palgrave Macmillan, pp. 185–203.

Faist, T., and Ette, A. (2007) *Between Autonomy and the European Union: The Europeanization of National Immigration Policies*. Basingstoke: Palgrave Macmillan.

Faist, T., and Fauser, M. (2011) The migration–development nexus: toward a transnational perspective, in T. Faist, M. Fauser and P. Kivisto (eds), *The Migration–Development Nexus: Transnational Perspectives*. Basingstoke: Palgrave Macmillan, pp. 1–26.

Faist, T., and Nergiz, D. (2012) Concluding remarks: considering contexts and units of analysis, in A. Amelina, D. Nergiz, T. Faist and N. Glick Schiller (eds), *Beyond Methodological Nationalism: Research Methodologies for Cross-Border Studies*. London: Routledge, pp. 239–44.

Faist, T., and Özveren, E. (eds), (2004) *Transnational Social Spaces: Agents, Networks and Institutions*. Aldershot: Ashgate.

Faist, T., and Ulbricht, C. (2013) Constituting national identity through transnationality: categorizations of inequality in German integration debates, in N. Foner and P. Simon (eds), *Fear and Anxiety over National Identity: Contrasting North American and European Experiences and Public Debates on Immigrant and Second Generation Integration*. New York: Russell Sage Foundation.

Faist, T., Fauser, M., and Reisenauer, E. (2011) Perspektiven der Migrationsforschung: Vom Transnationalismus zur Transnationalität, *Soziale Welt*, 62(2): 203–20.

Falzon, M.-A. (2009) *Multi-Sited Ethnography: Theory, Praxis and Locality in Contemporary Research*. Aldershot: Ashgate.

Fauser, M. (2011) How receiving cities contribute to simultaneous engagements for incorporation and development, in T. Faist, M. Fauser and P. Kivisto (eds), *The Migration–Development Nexus: Transnational Perspectives*. Basingstoke: Palgrave Macmillan, pp. 134–58.

Fauser, M. (2012) *Migrants and Cities: The Accommodation of Migrant Organizations in Europe*. Aldershot: Ashgate.

Fauser, M., and Reisenauer, E. (2012) Diversität und Dynamik transnationaler persönlicher Beziehungen türkischer MigrantInnen in Deutschland, in B. Pusch (ed.), *Transnationale Migration am Beispiel Deutschland und Türkei*. Wiesbaden: VS Verlag für Sozialwissenschaften, pp. 171–85.

Fenton, S. (2004) Beyond ethnicity: the global comparative analysis of ethnic conflict, *International Journal of Comparative Sociology*, 45(3–4): 179–94.

References

Findlay, A. (1995) Skilled transients: the invisible phenomenon?, in R. Cohen (ed.), *The Cambridge Survey of World Migration*. Cambridge: Cambridge University Press, pp. 515–22.

Fix, M., Papademetriou, D. G., Batalova, J., Terrazas, A., Yi-Ying Lin, S., and Mittelstadt, M. (2009) *Migration and the Global Recession*. Washington, DC: Migration Policy Institute.

Foner, N. (2001) Transnationalism then and now: New York immigrants today and at the turn of the twentieth century, in H. R. Cordero-Guzmán, R. C. Smith and R. Grosfoguel (eds), *Migration, Transnationalization, and Race in a Changing New York*. Philadelphia: Temple University Press, pp. 35–57.

Fouron, G. E., and Glick Schiller, N. (2001) The generation of identity: redefining the second generation within a transnational social field, in H. R. Cordero-Guzmán, R. C. Smith and R. Grosfoguel (eds), *Migration, Transnationalization, and Race in a Changing New York*. Philadelphia: Temple University Press, pp. 58–86.

Fox, J. (2005) Unpacking 'transnational citizenship', *Annual Review of Political Sciences*, 8: 171–201.

Fox, J. (2007) *Accountability Politics: Power and Voice in Rural Mexico*. New York: Oxford University Press, pp. 287–332.

Frank, A. G. (1978) *Dependent Accumulation and Underdevelopment*. London: Macmillan.

Freeman, G. P., and Ögelman, N. (1998) Homeland citizenship policies and the status of third country nationals in the European Union, *Journal of Ethnic and Migration Studies*, 24(4): 769–88.

Gamlen, A. (2008) The emigration state and the modern geopolitical imagination, *Political Geography*, 27(8): 840–56.

Gans, H. J. (1979) Symbolic ethnicity: the future of ethnic groups and cultures in America, in H. J. Gans (ed.), *On the Making of Americans*. University of Pennsylvania Press, Philadelphia, pp. 193–220.

Gans, H. J. (1992) Comment: ethnic invention and acculturation, a bumpy-line approach, *Journal of American Ethnic History*, 12(1): 42–52.

Gerdes, J., and Reisenauer, E. (2012) From return-oriented to integration-related transnationalisation: Turkish migrants in Germany, *Revue Européenne des Migrations Internationales*, 28(1): 107–28.

Gerdes, J., Reisenauer, E., and Sert, D. (2012) Varying transnational and multi-cultural activities in the Turkish–German migration context, in P. Pitkänen, A. Içduygu and D. Sert (eds), *Migration and Transformation: Multi-Level Analysis of Migrant Transnationalism*. New York and London: Springer, pp. 103–57.

Giddens, A. (1990) *The Consequences of Modernity*. Stanford, CA: Stanford University Press.

Glazer, N., and Moynihan, D. P. (1963) *Beyond the Melting Pot: The Negroes, Puerto Ricans, Jews, Italians and Irish of New York City*. Cambridge, MA: Harvard University Press.

References

Glick Schiller, N., and Fouron, G. (1999) Terrains of blood and nation: Haitian transnational social fields, *Ethnic and Racial Studies*, 22(2): 340–66.

Glick Schiller, N., Basch, L., and Blanc-Szanton, C. (1992a) Towards a definition of transnationalism: introductory remarks and research questions, in N. Glick Schiller, L. Basch and C. Blanc-Szanton (eds), *Towards a Transnational Perspective on Migration: Race, Class, Ethnicity, and Nationalism Reconsidered*. New York: New York Academy of Sciences, pp. ix–xiv.

Glick Schiller, N., Basch, L., and Blanc-Szanton, C. (1992b) Transnationalism: a new analytical framework for understanding migration, in N. Glick Schiller, L. Basch and C. Blanc-Szanton (eds), *Towards a Transnational Perspective on Migration: Race, Class, Ethnicity, and Nationalism Reconsidered*. New York: New York Academy of Sciences, pp. 1–24.

Glick Schiller, N., Basch, L., and Blanc-Szanton, C. (1994) *Nations Unbound: Transnational Projects, Postcolonial Predicaments, and Deterritorialized Nation-States*. Amsterdam: Gordon and Breach.

Glick Schiller, N., Çağlar, A., and Gulbrandsen, T. C. (2006) Beyond the ethnic lens: locality, globality and born-again incorporation. *American Ethnologist*, 33(4): 612–33.

Glick Schiller, N., Nieswand, B., Darieva, T., Yalcın-Heckmann, L., and Fostó, L. (2005) Pathways of migrant incorporation in Germany, *Transit* 1(1), http://repositories.cdlib.org/ucbgerman/transit/vol1/iss1/art50911 (accessed 5 January 2012).

Gold, S. J. (2002) *The Israeli Diaspora*. Seattle: University of Washington Press.

Goldring, L. (2004) Family and collective remittances to Mexico: a multi-dimensional typology of remittances, *Development and Change*, 35(4): 799–840.

Goldring, L., and Krishnamurti, G. (eds), (2007) *Organizing the Transnational: Labour, Politics, and Social Change*. Vancouver: University of British Columbia Press.

Gordon, M. M. (1964) *Assimilation in American Life: The Role of Race, Religion, and National Origin*. New York: Oxford University Press.

Gramsci, A. (1971) *Selections from the Prison Notebooks*. London: Lawrence & Wishart.

Grillo, R., and Riccio, B. (2004) Translocal development: Italy–Senegal, *Population, Space and Place*, 10(2): 99–111.

Guarnizo, L. E. (2003) The economics of transnational living, *International Migration Review*, 37(3): 666–99.

Guarnizo, L. E., Portes, A., and Haller, W. (2003) Assimilation and transnationalism: determinants of transnational political action among contemporary migrants, *American Journal of Sociology*, 108(6): 1211–48.

Guarnizo, L. E., and Díaz, L. M. (1999) Transnational migration: a view from Colombia, *Ethnic and Racial Studies*, 22(2): 397–421.

References

Ha, W., Yi, J., and Zhang, J. (2009) *Inequality and Internal Migration in China*, UNDP Human Development Research Paper 2009/27, http://hdr.undp.org/en/reports/global/hdr2009/papers/HDRP_2009_27.pdf (accessed 10 July 2012).

Hamilton, K., and Yau, J. (2004) The global tug-of-war for health care workers, *Migration Information Source: Fresh Thought, Autoritative Data, Global Reach*, www.migrationinformation.org/feature/display.cfm?ID=271 (accessed 31 July 2012).

Handlin, O. ([1951] 1973) *The Uprooted: The Epic Story of the Great Migrations that Made the American People*. 2nd edn, Boston: Little, Brown.

Harvey, D. (1990) *The Condition of Postmodernity: An Enquiry into the Origins of Cultural Change*. Oxford: Blackwell.

Haus, L. (2002) *Unions, Immigration and Internationalization: New Challenges and Changing Coalitions in the United States and France*. New York: Palgrave Macmillan.

Hegel, G. W. F. ([1822] 1991) *Elements of the Philosophy of Right*. Cambridge: Cambridge University Press.

Held, D., McGrew, A., Goldblatt, D., and Perraton, J. (1999) *Global Transformations: Politics, Economics and Culture*. Stanford, CA: Stanford University Press.

Hockenos, P. (2003) *Homeland Calling: Exile, Patriotism and the Balkan Wars*. Ithaca, NY: Cornell University Press.

Holst, E., Schäfer, A., and Schrooten, M. (2012) Gender and remittances: evidence from Germany, *Feminist Economics*, 18(2): 201–29.

Hondagneu-Sotelo, P. (2000) Feminism and migration, *Annals of the American Academy of Political and Social Science*, 571(1): 107–20.

Hondagneu-Sotelo, P., and Avila, E. (1997) 'I'm here, but I'm there': the meanings of Latina transnational motherhood, *Gender and Society*, 11(5): 548–71.

Horst, C. (2006) *Transnational Nomads: How Somalis Cope with Refugee Life in the Dadaab Camps of Kenya*. Oxford: Berghahn.

Hunger, U. (2003) Brain Drain oder Brain Gain Migration und Entwicklung, in D. Thränhardt and U. Hunger (eds), *Migration im Spannungsfeld von Globalisierung und Nationalstaat*. Wiesbaden: Westdeutscher Verlag, pp. 58–75.

Huntington, S. (2003) *Who Are We? The Challenges to America's National Identity*. New York: Simon & Schuster.

IOM (International Organization for Migration) (2005) *World Migration: Costs and Benefits of International Migration*. Geneva: IOM.

IOM (International Organization for Migration) (2009) *Summary World Migration Report 2010*, http://publications.iom.int/bookstore/free/WMR 2010_summary.pdf (accessed 10 July 2012).

Itzigsohn, J., and Saucedo, S. G. (2002) Immigrant incorporation and sociocultural transnationalism, *International Migration Review*, 36(3): 766–98.

References

Itzigsohn, J., and Saucedo, S. G. (2005) Incorporation, transnationalism, and gender: immigrant incorporation and transnational participation as gendered processes, *International Migration Review*, 39(4): 895–920.

Itzigsohn, J., and Villacrés, D. (2008) Migrant political transnationalism and the practice of democracy: Dominican external voting rights and Salvadoran home town associations, *Ethnic and Racial Studies*, 31(4): 664–86.

Itzigsohn, J., Dore Cabral, C., Hernandez Medina, E., and Vazquez, O. (1999) Mapping Dominican transnationalism: narrow and broad transnational practices, *Ethnic and Racial Studies*, 22(2): 316–39.

Jenkins, S. (ed.), (1988) *Ethnic Associations and the Welfare State: Services to Immigrants in Five Countries*. New York: Columbia University Press.

Jones, R. C. (1998) Remittances and inequality: a question of migration stage and geographic scale, *Economic Geography*, 74(1): 8–25.

Jones-Correa, M. (2002) The study of transnationalism among the children of immigrants: where we are and where we should be headed, in P. Levitt and M. C. Waters (eds), *The Changing Face of Home: The Transnational Lives of the Second Generation*. New York: Russell Sage Foundation, pp. 221–41.

Kallen, H. (1996) Democracy versus the melting pot: a study of American nationality, in W. Sollors (ed.), *Theories of Ethnicity: A Classical Reader*. Basingstoke: Palgrave Macmillan, pp. 67–92.

Kapur D. (2004) *Remittances: The New Development Mantra?*, G-24 Discussion Paper Series, no. 29. Washington, DC: World Bank.

Kapur, D. (2010) *Diaspora, Development, and Democracy: The Domestic Impact of International Migration from India*. Princeton, NJ: Princeton University Press.

Keane, J. (2003) *Global Civil Society*. Cambridge: Cambridge University Press.

Keck, M. E., and Sikkink, K. (1998) *Activists Beyond Borders: Advocacy Networks in International Politics*. Ithaca, NY: Cornell University Press.

Keohane, R. O., and Nye, J. S. (1977) *Power and Interdependence: World Politics in Transition*. Boston: Little, Brown.

Khadria, B. (2002) *Skilled Labour Migration from Developing Countries: Study on India*, International Migration Papers 49. Geneva: International Labour Office.

Khadria, B. (2009) Adversary analysis and the quest for global development: optimizing the dynamic conflict of interests in the transnational divide of migration, *Social Analysis*, 53(3): 106–22.

Khagram, S., and Levitt, P. (2008) Constructing transnational studies, in S. Khagram and P. Levitt (eds), *The Transnational Studies Reader: Intersections and Innovations*. London: Routledge, pp. 1–18.

King, R., and Christou, A. (2010a) Cultural geographies of counter-diasporic migration: perspectives from the study of second-generation 'returnees' to Greece, *Population, Space and Place*, 16(2): 103–19.

References

King, R., and Christou, A. (2010b) Diaspora, migration and transnationalism: insights from the study of second-generation 'returnees', in R. Bauböck and T. Faist (eds), *Diaspora and Transnationalism: Concepts, Theories and Methods*. Amsterdam: Amsterdam University Press, pp. 167–83.

Kissau, K., and Hunger, U. (2010) The internet as a means of studying transnationalism and diaspora, in R. Bauböck and T. Faist (eds), *Diaspora and Transnationalism: Concepts, Theories and Methodology*. Amsterdam: Amsterdam University Press, pp. 245–66.

Kivisto, P. (2001) Theorizing transnational immigration: a critical review of current efforts, *Ethnic and Racial Studies*, 24(4): 549–77.

Kivisto, P. (2003) Social spaces, transnational immigrant communities, and the politics of incorporation, *Ethnicities*, 3(1): 5–28.

Kivisto, P. (2005) The revival of assimilation in historical perspective, in P. Kivisto (ed.), *Incorporating Diversity: Rethinking Assimilation in a Multicultural Age*. Boulder, CO: Paradigm, pp. 3–29.

Kivisto, P., and Faist, T. (2010) *Beyond a Border: The Causes and Consequences of Contemporary Immigration*. Thousand Oaks, CA: Pine Forge Press.

Koinova, M. (2010) Diasporas and international politics: utilising the universalistic creed of liberalism for particularistic and nationalist purposes, in R. Bauböck and T. Faist (eds), *Diaspora and Transnationalism: Concepts, Theories and Methods*. Amsterdam: Amsterdam University Press, pp. 149–66.

Koser, L. (ed.) (2003) *New African Diasporas*. London: Routledge.

Kymlicka, W. (1995) *Multicultural Citizenship: A Liberal Theory of Minority Rights*. Oxford : Oxford University Press.

Lacroix, T. (2005) *Les Réseaux marocains du développement: géographie du transnational et politiques du territorial*. Paris : Presses de la Fondation nationale des sciences politiques.

Lafleur, J. M. (2011) Why do states enfranchise citizens abroad? Comparative insights from Mexico, Italy and Belgium, *Global Networks*, 11(4): 1–21.

Laguerre, M. (1998) *Diasporic Citizenship: Haitian Americans in Transnational America*. Basingstoke: Macmillan.

Landolt, P., and Da, W. W. (2005) The spatially ruptured practices of migrant families: a comparison of immigrants from El Salvador and the People's Republic of China, *Current Sociology*, 53(4): 625–53.

Landolt, P. (2001) Salvadoran economic transnationalism: embedded strategies for household maintenance, immigrant incorporation, and entrepreneurial expansion, *Global Networks*, 1(3): 217–41.

Layton-Henry, Z. (1990) Immigrant associations, in Z. Layton-Henry (ed.), *The Political Rights of Migrant Workers in Western Europe*. London: Sage, pp. 94–112.

Leichtmann, M. (2005) The legacy of transnational lives: beyond the first generation of Lebanese in Senegal, *Ethnic and Racial Studies*, 28(4): 663–86.

References

Levitt, P. (1997) Transnationalizing community development: the case of migration between Boston and the Dominican Republic, *Nonprofit and Voluntary Sector Quarterly*, 26(4): 509–26.

Levitt, P. (1998) Social remittances: migration driven local-level forms of cultural diffusion, *International Migration Review*, 32(4): 926–48.

Levitt, P. (2001a) *The Transnational Villagers*. Berkeley: University of California Press.

Levitt, P. (2001b) Transnational migration: taking stock and future directions, *Global Networks*, 1(3): 195–216.

Levitt, P. (2002) The ties that change: relations to the ancestral home over the life cycle, in P. Levitt and M. C. Waters (eds), *The Changing Face of Home: The Transnational Lives of the Second Generation*. New York: Russell Sage Foundation, pp. 123–44.

Levitt, P. (2003) Keeping feet in both worlds: transnational practices and immigrant incorporation in the United States, in C. Joppke and E. Morawska (eds), *Toward Assimilation and Citizenship: Immigrants in Liberal Nation-States*. Basingstoke: Palgrave Macmillan, pp. 177–94.

Levitt, P. (2007) *God Needs No Passport: Immigrants and the Changing American Religious Landscape*. New York: New Press.

Levitt, P. (2011) Constructing gender across borders: a transnational approach, in E. N.-L. Chow, M. T. Segal and L. Tan (eds), *Analyzing Gender, Intersectionality, and Multiple Inequalities: Global, Transnational and Local Contexts*. Bingley: Emerald.

Levitt, P., and Glick Schiller, N. (2004) Conceptualizing simultaneity: a transnational social field perspective on society, *International Migration Review*, 38(3): 1002–39.

Levitt, P., and Jaworsky, B. N. (2007) Transnational migration studies: past developments and future trends, *Annual Review of Sociology*, 33: 129–56.

Levitt, P. & Waters, M. C. (eds) (2002) *The Changing Face of Home: The Transnational Lives of the Second Generation*. New York: Russell Sage Foundation.

Levitt, P., DeWind, J., and Vertovec, S. (2003) International perspectives on transnational migration: an introduction, *International Migration Review*, 37(3): 565–75.

Linz, J. J., and Stepan, A. (1996) *Problems of Democratic Transition and Consolidation: Southern Europe, South America, and Post-Communist Europe*. Baltimore: John Hopkins University Press.

Lipton, M. (1980) Migration from rural areas of poor countries: the impact on rural productivity and income distribution, *World Development*, 8(1): 1–24.

Lowell, L. B., Findlay, A., and Stewart, E. (2004) *Brain Strain: Optimising Highly Skilled Migration from Developing Countries*, Asylum and Working Paper 4. London: Institute for Public Policy Research.

References

Lutz, H., and Palenga-Möllenbeck, E. (2012) Care workers, care drain, and care chains: reflections on care, migration, and citizenship, *Social Politics*, 19(1): 15–37.

Madianou, M., and Miller, D. (2012) *Migration and New Media: Transnational Families and Polymedia*. London: Routledge.

Mahler, S. (1998) Theoretical and empirical contributions toward a research agenda for transnationalism, in P. M. Smith and L. E. Guarnizo (eds), *Transnationalism from Below*. New Brunswick, NJ: Transaction Books, pp. 64–102.

Marcus, G. (1995) Ethnography in/of the world system: the emergence of multi-sited ethnography, *Annual Review of Anthropology*, 24(1): 95–117.

Marshall, T. H. ([1950] 1964) *Citizenship and Social Class*. Cambridge: Cambridge University Press.

Martiniello, M., and Rath, J. (eds) (2010) *Selected Studies in International Migration and Immigrant Incorporation*. Amsterdam: Amsterdam University Press.

Martins, H. (1974) Time and theory in sociology, in J. Rex (ed.), *Approaches to Sociology: An Introduction to Major Trends in British Sociology*. London: Routledge & Kegan Paul, pp. 246–94.

Marx, K., and Engels, F. ([1845] 2011) *The German Ideology*. London: Lawrence & Wishart.

Massey, D. (1987) The ethnosurvey in theory and practice, *International Migration Review*, 21(4): 1498–522.

Massey, D. (2008) *For Space*. 2nd edn, London: Sage.

Mau, S. (2007) *Transnationale Vergesellschaftung*. Frankfurt am Main: Campus.

Mau, S. (2010) *Social Transnationalism: Lifeworlds beyond the Nation-State*. London: Routledge.

Mazzucato, V. (2006) Migrant transnationalism: two-way flows, changing institutions and community development between Ghana and the Netherlands, *Economic Sociology: The European Electronic Newsletter*, 7(3): 8–17.

Mazzucato, V. (2008) Simultaneity and networks in transnational migration: lessons learned from a simultaneous matched sample methodology, in J. DeWind and J. Holdaway (eds), *Migration and Development within and across Borders: Research and Policy Perspectives on Internal and International Migration*. Geneva: International Organization for Migration, pp. 69–100.

Mazzucato, V., and Schans, D. (2011) Transnational families and the well-being of children: conceptual and methodological challenges, *Journal of Marriage and Family*, 73(4): 704–12.

Mercer, C., Page, B., and Evans, M. (2009) Unsettling connections: transnational networks, development and African home associations, *Global Networks*, 9(2): 141–61.

Meyer, J.-B. (2001) Network Approach versus brain drain lessons from the diaspora, *International Migration*, 39(5): 91–110.

References

Meyer, J.-B. (2011) A sociology of diaspora knowledge networks, in T. Faist, M. Fauser and P. Kivisto (eds), *The Migration–Development Nexus: A Transnational Perspective*. Basingstoke: Palgrave Macmillan, pp. 159–84.

Meyer, J.-B., Charum, J., Bernal, D., Gaillard, J., Granés, J., Leon, J., Montenegro, A., Morales, A., Murcia, C., Narvaez-Berthelemot, N., Parrado, L. S., and Schlemmer, B. (1997) Turning brain drain into brain gain: the Colombian experience of the diaspora option, *Science, Technology and Society*, 2(2): 285–315.

Morales, L., and Jorba, L. (2010) The transnational links and practices of migrants' organisations in Spain, in R. Bauböck and T. Faist (eds), *Transnationalism and Diaspora: Concepts, Theories and Methods*. Amsterdam: Amsterdam University Press, pp. 267–93.

Morawska, E. (2003) Immigrant transnationalism and assimilation: a variety of combinations and the analytic strategy it suggests, in C. Joppke and E. Morawska (eds), *Toward Assimilation and Citizenship: Immigrants in Liberal Nation-States*. Basingstoke: Palgrave Macmillan, pp. 133–76.

Moya, J. C. (2005) Immigrants and associations: a global and historical perspective, *Journal of Ethnic and Migration Studies*, 31(5): 833–64.

Naïr, S. (1997) *Rapport de bilan et d'orientations sur la politique de co-développement liée aux flux migratoires*. Paris: Premier Ministre.

Newland, K., and Tanaka, H. (2010) *Mobilizing Diaspora Entrepreneurship for Development*. Washington, DC: Migration Policy Institute.

Nyberg-Sørensen, N., Van Hear, N., and Engberg-Pedersen, P. (2002) *The Migration–Development Nexus: Evidence and Policy Options*. IOM Migration Research Series 8. Geneva: International Organization for Migration.

OECD (2009) Development aid at its highest level in 2008, *International Development Statistics online*, at: www.oecd.org (accessed 27 February 2012).

Orozco, M., and Lapointe, M. (2004) Mexican hometown associations and development opportunities, *Journal of International Affairs*, 57(2): 31–51.

Østergaard-Nielsen, E. (2001) Transnational political practices and the receiving state: Turks and Kurds in Germany and the Netherlands, *Global Networks*, 1(3): 261–81.

Østergaard-Nielsen, E. (2003a) The politics of migrants' transnational political practices, *International Migration Review*, 37(3): 760–86.

Østergaard-Nielsen, E. (2003b) *Transnational Politics: Turks and Kurds in Germany*. London and New York: Routledge.

Park, R. E. (1928) Human migration and the marginal man, *American Journal of Sociology*, 33(6): 881–93.

Parreñas, R. S. (2001a) Mothering from a distance: emotions, gender, and intergenerational relations in Filipino transnational families, *Feminist Studies*, 27(2): 361–90.

Parreñas, R. S. (2001b) *Servants of Globalization: Women, Migration, and Domestic Work*. Stanford, CA: Stanford University Press.

References

Pérez-Armendáriz, C., and Crow, D. (2010) Do migrants remit democracy? International migration, political beliefs, and behavior in Mexico, *Comparative Political Studies*, 43(1): 119–48.

Piperno, F. (2007) From care drain to care gain: migration in Romania and Ukraine and the rise of transnational welfare, *Development*, 50: 63–68.

Pitkänen, P., and Kalekin-Fishman, D. (2007) *Multiple State Membership and Citizenship in an Era of Transnational Migration*. Rotterdam: Sense.

Pitkänen, P., Içduygu, A., and Sert, D. (eds) (2012) *Migration and Transformation: Multi-Level Analysis of Migrant Transnationalism*. New York and London: Springer.

Polanyi, K. ([1944] 2001) *The Great Transformation: The Political and Economic Origins of our Time*. 2nd edn, Boston: Beacon Press.

Portes, A. (1996) Transnational communities: their emergence and significance in the contemporary world-system, in R. P. Korzeniewicz and W. C. Smith (eds), *Latin America in the World-Economy*. Westport, CT: Greenwood Press, pp. 151–68.

Portes, A. (2001) Introduction: the debates and significance of immigrant trans-nationalism, *Global Networks*, 1(3): 181–93.

Portes, A. (2003) Conclusion: theoretical convergencies and empirical evidence in the study of immigrant transnationalism, *International Migration Review*, 37(3): 874–92.

Portes, A., and Rumbaut, R. G. (2001) *Legacies: The Story of the Immigrant Second Generation*. Berkeley: University of California Press.

Portes, A., and Zhou, M. (1993) The new second generation: segmented assimilation and its variants, *Annals of the American Academy of Political and Social Science*, 530(1): 74–96.

Portes, A., Escobar, C., and Arana, R. (2008) Bridging the gap: transnational and ethnic organizations in the political incorporation of immigrants in the United States, *Ethnic and Racial Studies*, 31(6): 1025–55.

Portes, A., Escobar, C., and Walton Radford, A. (2007) Immigrant transnational organizations and development: a comparative study, *International Migration Review*, 41(1): 242–81.

Portes, A., Guarnizo, L. E., and Haller, W. (2003) Assimilation and transnationalism: determinants of transnational political action among contemporary migrants, *American Journal of Sociology*, 108(6): 1211–48.

Portes, A., Guarnizo, L. E., and Landolt, P. (1999) The study of transnationalism: pitfalls and promise of an emergent research field, *Ethnic and Racial Studies*, 22(2): 217–37.

Portes, A., Haller, W., and Guarnizo, L. E. (2002) Transnational entrepreneurs: an alternative form of immigrant economic adaption, *American Sociological Review*, 67(2): 278–98.

References

Ratha, R., and Shaw, W. (2007) *South–South Migration and Remittances*, http://siteresources.worldbank.org/INTPROSPECTS/Resources/South-Southmigrationjan192006.pdf (accessed 10 July 2012).

Reichert, J. S. (1981) The migrant syndrome: seasonal US labour migration and rural development in Central Mexico, *Human Organization*, 40(1): 56–66.

Rex, J., Joly, D., and Wilpert, C. (1987) *Immigrant Associations in Europe*. Aldershot: Gower.

Rivera-Salgado, G. (1999) Mixtec activism in Oaxacalifornia: transborder grassroots political strategies, *American Behavioral Scientist*, 42(9): 1439–58.

Rushdie, S. (1991) *Imaginary Homelands*. London: Granta Books.

Sassen, S. (2002) Global cities and diasporic networks: microsites in global civil society, in M. Glasius, M. Kaldor and H. Anheier (eds), *Global Civil Society Yearbook*. Oxford and New York: Oxford University Press, pp. 217–38.

Saxenian, A. (2004) The Silicon Valley connection: transnational networks and regional development in Taiwan, China and India, in A. D'Costa and E. Sridharan (eds), *India in the Global Software Industry: Innovation, Firm Strategies and Development*. Basingstoke: Palgrave Macmillan.

Schmidt, G. (2011) Law and identity: transnational arranged marriages and the boundaries of Danishness, *Journal of Ethnic and Migration Studies*, 37(2): 257–75.

Schmitter Heisler, B. (1985) Sending countries and the politics of emigration and destination, *International Migration Review*, 19(3): 469–84.

Schröter, Y., and Jäger, R. (2007) We are children of Europe: multiple citizenship in Germany, in P. Pitkänen and D. Kalekin-Fishman (eds), *Multiple State Membership and Citizenship in an Era of Transnational Migration*. Rotterdam: Sense, pp. 67–90.

Shain, J. (1999) *Marketing the American Creed Abroad*. Cambridge: Cambridge University Press.

Shain, Y., and Barth, A. (2003) Diasporas and international relations theory, *International Organization*, 57(3): 449–79.

Shelley, L. (1995) Transnational organized crime: an imminent threat to the nation-state? *Journal of International Affairs*, 48(2): 463–91.

Sieveking, N. (2011) 'We are not equal!' Methodological reflections on conducting research on migrants as development actors, in T. Faist and N. Sieveking (eds), *Unravelling Migrants as Transnational Agents of Development: Social Spaces in Between Ghana and Germany*. Münster: Lit, pp. 187–218.

Sieveking, N., and Fauser, M. (2009) *Migrationsdynamiken und Entwicklung in Westafrika: Untersuchungen zur entwicklungspolitischen Bedeutung von Migration in und aus Ghana und Mali*, working paper 68/2009. Bielefeld: Centre on Migration, Citizenship and Development.

References

Sieveking, N., Fauser, M., and Faist, T. (2008) *Gutachten zum entwicklungspolitischen Engagement der in NRW lebenden MigrantInnen afrikanischer Herkunft*, working paper 28/2008. Bielefeld: Centre on Migration, Citizenship and Development.

Singelton, A. (1999) Combining quantitative and qualitative research methods in the study of international migration, *International Journal of Social Research Methodology*, 2(2): 151–7.

Sklair, L. (2001) *The Transnational Capitalist Class*. Oxford: Blackwell.

Smith, L. (2011) Business as usual? Urban actors and transnational investments in Accra, Ghana, in T. Faist, M. Fauser and P. Kivisto (eds), *The Migration–Development Nexus: A Transnational Perspective*. Basingstoke: Palgrave Macmillan, pp. 104–33.

Smith, M. P. (2007) The two faces of transnational citizenship, *Ethnic and Racial Studies*, 30(6): 1096–116.

Smith, M. P., and Bakker, M. (2005) The transnational politics of the tomato king: meaning and impact, *Global Networks*, 5(2): 129–46.

Smith, R. (2003) Diasporic memberships in historical perspective: comparative insights from the Mexican, Italian and Polish cases, *International Migration Review*, 37(3): 724–59.

Snel, E., Engbergsen, G., and Leerkes, A. (2006) Transnational involvement and social integration, *Global Networks*, 6(3): 285–308.

Stark, O. (1991) Migration in LDCs: risk, remittances, and the family, *Finance and Development*, 28(4): 39–41.

Stark, O., and Lucas, R. E. B. (1988) Migration, remittances and the family, *Economic Development and Cultural Change*, 36(3): 465–81.

Stilwell, B., Diallo, K., Zurn, P., Vujicic, M., Adams, O., and Dal Poz, M. (2004) Migration of health-care workers from developing countries: strategic approaches to its management, *Bulletin of the World Health Organization*, 82(8): 595–600.

Strassburger, G. (2004) Transnational ties of the second generation: marriages of Turks in Germany, in T. Faist and E. Özveren (eds), *Transnational Social Spaces: Agents, Networks and Institutions*. Aldershot: Ashgate, pp. 211–31.

Tarrow, S. (2005) *The New Transnational Activism*. Cambridge: Cambridge University Press.

Tejada Guerrero, G., and Bolay, J.-C. (2005) *Enhancing Development through Knowledge Circulation: A Different View of the Migration of Highly Skilled Mexicans*. Geneva: Global Commission on International Migration.

Thomas, W. I., and Znaniecki, F. (1918–20) *The Polish Peasant in Europe and America*, 5 vols. Vols. 1–2, Chicago: University of Chicago Press; Vols. 3–5, Boston: Richard G. Badger.

Thomson, M., and Crul, M. (2007) The second generation in Europe and the United States: how is the transatlantic debate relevant for further research on the European second generation? *Journal of Ethnic and Migration Studies*, 33(7): 1025–41.

Tilly, C. (2005) *Identities, Boundaries and Social Ties*. Boulder, CO: Paradigm.

Tocqueville, A. de ([1835] 1988) *Democracy in America*, ed. J. P. Mayer, trans. G. Lawrence. New York: Harper & Row.

Tsuda, T. (2003) *Strangers in the Ethnic Homeland: Japanese Brazilian Return Migration in Transnational Perspective*. New York: Columbia University Press.

Turner, B. S. (2001) The erosion of citizenship, *British Journal of Sociology*, 52(2): 189–210.

UN (2009) *International Migration*, www.un.org/esa/population/publications/2009Migration_Chart/ittmig_wallchart09.pdf (accessed 10 July 2012).

UNDP (2009) *Human Development Report 2009: Overcoming Barriers: Human Mobility and Development*. Basingstoke: Palgrave Macmillan.

Van Hear, N. (2011) Diasporas, recovery and development in conflict-ridden societies, in T. Faist, M. Fauser and P. Kivisto (eds), *The Migration–Development Nexus: A Transnational Perspective*. Basingstoke: Palgrave Macmillan, pp. 85–103.

Vertovec, S. (2004) Migrant transnationalism and modes of transformation, *International Migration Review*, 38(3): 970–1001.

Vertovec, S. (2009) *Transnationalism*. London: Routledge.

Waldinger, R., Popkin, E., and Magana, H. A. (2008) Conflict and contestation in the cross-border community: hometown associations reassessed, *Ethnic and Racial Studies*, 31(5): 843–70.

Wallerstein, I. (1974) *The Modern World-System*. New York: Academic Press.

Walzer, M. (1989) Citizenship, in T. Ball, J. Farr and R. L. Hanson (eds), *Political Innovation and Conceptual Change*. Cambridge: Cambridge University Press, pp. 211–20.

Warner, W. L., and Srole, L. (1947) *The Social Systems of American Ethnic Groups*. New Haven, CT: Yale University Press.

Weber, M. ([1904] 1959) *The Protestant Ethic and the Spirit of Capitalism*. New York: Scribner's.

Webber, M. M. (1963) Order in diversity: community without propinquity, in L. Wingo (ed.), *Cities and Space: The Future Use of Urban Land*. Baltimore: Johns Hopkins University Press, pp. 23–54.

Wimmer, A., and Glick Schiller, N. (2003) Methodological nationalism, the social sciences, and the study of migration: an essay in historical epistemology, *International Migration Review*, 37(3): 576–610.

World Bank (2008) *Migration and Remittances Factbook 2008*, www-wds.worldbank.org/external/default/WDSContentServer/IW3P/IB/2008/03/14/000333038 _ 20080314060040 / Rendered / PDF / 429130PUB0Migr101OFFICIAL0USE0ONLY1.pdf (accessed 31 July 2012).

References

World Bank (2009) *Migration and Remittance Trends 2009*, Migration and Development Brief 11. Washington, DC: World Bank.

World Bank (2011) *Migration and Remittances Factbook 2011*. 2nd edn, Washington, DC: World Bank.

Yeates, N. (2009) *Globalizing Care Economies and Migrant Workers: Explorations in Global Care Chains*. Basingstoke: Palgrave Macmillan.

Zabin, C., and Escala, L. (2002) From civic association to political participation: Mexican hometown associations and Mexican immigrant political empowerment in Los Angeles, *Frontera Norte*, 14(27): 1–34.

Zaiotti, R. (2011) *Cultures of Border Control: Schengen and the Evolution of European Frontiers*. Chicago: University of Chicago Press.

Zechner, M. (2008) Care of older persons in transnational settings, *Journal of Aging Studies*, 22(1): 32–44.

Zhou, M. (2004) Revisiting ethnic entrepreneurship: convergencies, controversies, and conceptual advancements, *International Migration Review*, 38(3): 1040–74.

Zolberg, A. R., and Woon, L. L. (1999) Why Islam is like Spanish: cultural incorporation in Europe and the United States, *Politics and Society*, 27(1): 5–38.

Index

Index

CPSIA information can be obtained
at www.ICGtesting.com
Printed in the USA
FSHW012250220120
66301FS